THE AUTHOR

Olive Brennan is a graduate of University College Dublin and the Honourable Society of King's Inns. A qualified teacher, she worked for Dublin Corporation before being called to the Bar. She is a barrister and a part-time lecturer at the College of Commerce, Rathmines, where she lectures in Business and Commercial Law.

LAYING DOWN THE LAW

A PRACTICAL GUIDE

LAYING DOWN THE LAW

A PRACTICAL GUIDE

Olive Brennan
BA. Barrister-at-Law

With a foreword by
His Honour Judge Liam Devally

Illustrations by Michael Moriarty

DUBLIN & CORK

This book was typeset by CORK PUBLISHING for Oak Tree Press, Granary House, Rutland Street, Cork and Ormond Court, 11 Lower Ormond Quay, Dublin 1.

British Library Cataloguing in Publication Data

A CIP Catalogue record for this book is available from the British Library.

ISBN 1 872853 04 8

Printed in Ireland by Colour Books Limited.

CONTENTS

FOREWORD

This book is essential reading. It is educational and informative. It explains the legal process not only to the casual reader, but also to the prospective plaintiff, defendant, prosecutor, or accused.

For the prospective litigant, it is a helpful compass, showing what being involved in court actions can entail.

For practitioners, solicitors and barristers alike, it is a salutary reminder of aspects of their work which are enormously important to their clients, but which can be overlooked on occasions, due to time pressures or the taking for granted of procedures with which the layperson is unfamiliar. An extra explanatory word or two during a consultation will never go astray, and can set a client's mind at rest.

For the family book-shelf, this book is a citizen's advice bureau and a consumer's advice service rolled into one. It is likely to be popular in both public and school libraries.

The style and perspective adopted by Olive Brennan is most refreshing and she deserves a wide readership. I have no doubt but that she will achieve this.

LIAM DEVALLY
September 1991

DISCLAIMER

This book has been prepared with the aim of providing the lay person with information about the law and how the Irish legal system works. It does not purport to be an exhaustive text on Irish law.

Oak Tree Press and the author accept no liability from anyone who relies solely on the material contained in this book.

We strongly recommend that readers should consult a solicitor before taking any action that may have legal consequences.

INTRODUCTION

Ignorance of the law makes people afraid — afraid of the legal system, afraid of going to court, afraid of judges, and afraid of dealing with legal advisers. This should not be so. The law is there to serve you.

At its best, the law exists to reconcile your differences, to compensate you for your loss or injuries, and to provide solutions to your legal problems. At its worst, the law is threatening and intimidating.

The need to know is a very basic need and you need to know about the law. My purpose in writing this book is to try to take the fear of the unknown out of the law.

This book is a practical and informative guide to the most common legal problems you may encounter at some stage of your life.

The aim of the book is to tell you simply and clearly how the law works in various situations, the remedies that may be available, together with practical advice which will help you to help your legal advisers.

This book is not a substitute for legal advice nor is it a DIY guide to law. In all legal matters, the best advice — and the only advice — is to consult a solicitor, sooner rather than later.

Olive Brennan
1 September 1991

To my Mother and the memory of Eamonn.

ACKNOWLEDGEMENTS

This book is the product of not just my own efforts, but of the help, advice and encouragement of a great many people.

I am most grateful to His Honour Judge Liam Devally for his gracious foreword.

Thanks is also due to my colleagues in the Law Library who read various chapters, made very helpful suggestions and pointed out the error of my ways: Peter Charleton BL and Mary O'Toole BL. Jane Barron BL and Yvonne Lynch BL did the same and more — they read the proofs not once but twice. I am most grateful to Andrew Bradley, Senior Counsel for his advice and counsel.

Thanks is also due to the Courts staff and in particular Ciaran Kelly BL, President's Registrar, Grainne O'Loghlen BL, Master's Registrar, Annette O'Connell BL, and James Finn BL of the Probate Office.

I owe a great deal of gratitude to Paula Duffy, solicitor, my friend and colleague, for the help and assistance throughout.

I am indebted to the staff of the Law Library, and the Library staff of the Honourable Society of King's Inns for their assistance.

I am very much aware that while the law can be theoretically correct the actual practice can, on occasions be somewhat different. Bearing that in mind, I sent various parts of the manuscript to experts in the field concerned. The assistance and advice of the personnel involved is very much appreciated. In particular I would like to thank Leo Crehan, BE, MIE, C.ENG, MIEI, MICE, Senior Building Surveyor in the Building Control Section of Dublin Corporation, Berna Grist BL, Chartered Town Planner, Ray Kerr BL, Dip. Eur. Law., of the Department of Industry and Commerce, Seamas Glynn, Chief Executive of the Irish Travel Agents Association, Junior Liason Officers Ken Hill and Dave Watts of Kevin Street Garda station.

A very special thanks is due to Finola O'Sullivan of

Butterworth (Ireland) Ltd. for making it happen. Rory O'Donnell, Solicitor made very many helpful comments and suggestions. I am most thankful to Emer Dignam and Jackie Murdoch for their work on the manuscript.

My family deserve enormous thanks for their love and support throughout.

My publisher Gerard O'Connor of Oak Tree Press was most patient.

Last but not least I would like to record a very sincere thank you to Dom Carroll, a friend, a guide and a mentor.

OLIVE BRENNAN
1st September, 1991

1

ACCIDENTS

We can all be wise with the benefit of hindsight. What we should have done, and what we did not do, can come back to haunt us long after the event. Being involved in a road traffic accident is a most unpleasant and unfortunate experience. It is also a very common occurrence.

WHAT TO DO AT THE SCENE OF AN ACCIDENT
You *must*:
- stop. You are obliged by law to do so;
- call the Gardaí to the scene of the accident, if anybody is injured;
- give the following information to the Gardaí:
  — your name and address;
  — the name and address of the owner of the car, if it is not your own;
  — the registration number of the car;
  — details of your insurance cover;
- report the accident to the Gardaí as soon as possible, if no Garda comes to the scene.

You *should*:
- keep your car at the scene of the accident for a reasonable period of time. If the car is causing an obstruction, or is a danger to other road users, you may move it but you should note its position:
- *do the following:*
  — obtain the name, address, and telephone number of the driver of the other car involved;
  — obtain the registration number and details of the insurance cover of the other car involved. This will

be available on the windscreen beside the tax disc (assuming that the windscreen is still in one piece after the accident);

— obtain the name, address and telephone number of any witnesses to the accident;

— take note of the driving conditions at the moment of impact (for example, wet, dark, broken down surface, details of any road markings and the lighting in the area);

— take note of the name of the Garda (if one arrives on the scene), his number, and station address;

• notify your own insurers of the accident as soon as possible. Do this in writing, not by telephone.

You *should not*:

• ever, under any circumstances, apologise or make any admissions of liability to the driver of the other car. Neither is it advisable to make an offer to repair any damage to the other car.

As a result of the accident, the investigating Garda may decide to prosecute either or both parties for dangerous or careless, or even reckless driving. If the investigating Garda subsequently calls looking for a statement from you, you are not obliged to give one. If you receive a notice of intention to prosecute from the Gardaí, you should immediately notify your insurers and contact a solicitor.

CAR REPAIRS

What should you do about having your car repaired after an accident?

You should get an estimate of what it will cost to repair. If it is not economical to repair the car (that is, if the car is a write-off), you should ask your garage for an estimate of pre-accident/post-accident value. The insurers of the driver of the other car (known as the third party) should be given reasonable notice to arrange to inspect the car before any repairs are carried out. If you are comprehensively insured, your own insurance company will want to inspect the car.

The terms of your insurance policy may allow you to hire a car, while your car is off the road. Check with your insurance company.

If the car is not inspected within a reasonable period, you can proceed with the repairs, but the damaged parts must be left aside for inspection later. In some cases, insurance companies agree a figure for car repairs directly with the garage.

PERSONAL INJURIES

Let us assume that, as a result of your accident, you have been injured. You have suffered pain, inconvenience and a lot of expense. Medical bills are mounting, the car has to be repaired, you may be out of work as a result of the accident and your earnings are down. You feel that you should be compensated for all of your losses and injuries.

WHAT SHOULD YOU DO?

The sequence which follows applies to all personal injury matters, whether as a result of a car accident or an accident at work, slipping and falling in a shop, or tripping and falling into a pot-hole in the street.

INSTRUCTING A SOLICITOR

The first thing you must do once you have recovered sufficiently from the accident is to see a solicitor. However you choose a solicitor – whether as a result of a personal recommendation, or because he or she practices in your area, or from the Golden Pages – it is usual to phone for an appointment, although if you would rather call in, the receptionist will make an appointment for you.

COSTS

Your solicitor will advise you of the costs involved in your case. If you are successful in your action, you will be awarded an amount for your injuries and the losses you incurred as a result of your accident. You will also be awarded some of the costs involved in taking the action. However, even if you are successful, there are some costs which the other side will not pay. These come under the heading of solicitor and client costs, and can include consultations with your legal advisers, or additional reports that the other side will not agree to pay. You are liable to pay these to your solicitor yourself. You will be given full details of such costs when taking the action.

If you lose your case, you will end up paying not only for your own costs but for the costs of the other side as well.

Having had an accident, it can be very upsetting to be told that you do not have a case. If you insist on taking an action against the other person against the best advice, it may cost you a lot of money. If you decide to go ahead with such an action, despite advice to the contrary from your solicitor, you may be asked for money in advance. Principles at law cost money, usually your own.

INFORMATION A SOLICITOR NEEDS

Time is money – your money. The clock begins to tick the moment you walk through your solicitor's door. Remember it is not a social visit, it is business. Your initial visit will be a fact-finding exercise as to the merits of your case.

Let us assume you were involved in a road traffic accident. Below is a series of questions. Your answers will assist your solicitor in deciding whether you have a case:
- where did the accident happen?
- when did the accident happen?
- what time?
- where were you coming from?
- where were you going to?
- what happened?
- what caused the accident?
- what were the weather conditions?
- what are the insurance details of the other car?
- what are the names and addresses of witnesses to the accident (if any)?
- what is the name of the investigating garda?
- what is the name of the garda station to which the accident was reported?

- what road markings were at the scene of the accident?
- what road signs were at the scene?
- what colour were the traffic lights (if there were traffic lights at the scene of the accident)?
- what injuries did you suffer?
- what treatment did you have?
- what doctor(s) treated you?
- is your treatment continuing?
- what costs did you incur?
- what are the details of your own insurance cover?

TIME LIMITS FOR TAKING AN ACTION
If you suffer personal injuries as a result of any accident, in the usual course of events, you have three years from the date of the accident to bring an action to court, except where the injured party is a minor or a person of diminished responsibility.

NEGLIGENCE
Just because you have been involved in an accident does not mean that somebody else will be liable to pay compensation to you for your injuries. In order to sue someone, they must have been at fault. Depending on the circumstances of the accident, you yourself may have caused or contributed in some way to the accident. If this is so, then although your action might be successful, the judge might find you guilty of contributory negligence and reduce your award by the percentage of blame attributed to your actions by the court. For example, if you were found to be fifty percent to blame for the accident, your award would be reduced by half.

THE SYSTEM OF COMPENSATION
Basically, your claim for compensation is divided into two parts:
- **general damages**: This is for the pain, suffering and inconvenience you had as a result of your injuries;
- **special damages**, referred to as *specials*. Specials include the costs and expense incurred as a result of the injuries, such as the cost of repair to a motor vehicle, hospital

5

expenses, physiotherapy, chemist's bills, the cost of travelling expenses, damage to your clothing and, in some instances, the cost of domestic help due to your incapacity as a result of your accident.

You will be asked to produce vouchers and receipts for any claim for special damages. It is most important that you keep all bills and receipts if you want to recover these costs. If you are claiming for loss of wages, your solicitor will need the name and address of your employer, together with your Social Welfare number (this should appear as your RSI number on your pay-slip).

A DIARY
Depending on the nature of your case, it may well be a long time before the matter comes for hearing in court. If your injuries are continuing, it is a good idea to keep a daily diary of your progress. With the passage of time, pain and discomfort blurs. It is normal that you would want to forget about it and put it all behind you. It can be difficult to recall exactly how you were feeling some two to three years after the event. A diary would be a great help to your medical advisers when you are re-examined before the court case.
  Write down:
- your original symptoms;
- your initial pain and discomfort;
- the medication you were prescribed;
- the dates of your visits to hospital for treatment;
- the dates of your visits for review;
- a personal account of how you coped and felt, as you went along.

HOW LONG WILL AN ACTION TAKE?
It depends on the nature of your case and on the nature of your injuries. After your initial visit, the solicitor will investigate the matter on your behalf.
  Initially, what is known as a letter before action will be sent to the other side stating your version of events, and asking them

to compensate you for the losses you have suffered. Various reports may have to be completed by different experts. For example, an engineer's report on the condition of the accident location may be necessary. Photographs may be taken of the scene of the accident for future evidence in court, in case repair or other works are carried out in the meantime. A specialist's report may be necessary on your injuries and your future prognosis. The Garda who investigated the accident will be contacted and the Garda report, which usually includes a sketch map of the accident together with any witness statements, may also be requested by your solicitor.

The reply to your solicitor's letter before action will usually be in one of two forms:

- the other side will accept that they were responsible for your accident and will offer to settle your claim without the necessity of going to Court;
- they will deny responsibility, in which case the matter may end up in court.

SETTLING A CLAIM

If the other side admits responsibility or liability for your injuries, and if your solicitor advises you to settle, then the solicitor will enter into negotiations on your behalf. If a mutually agreed figure can be reached, that is the end of the matter and the case proceeds no further.

Settlement can occur anytime up to and including the day of the court hearing. If a settlement is proposed, you may be invited by your solicitor to attend what is known as a settlement consultation.

Settlement consultations are usually arranged for the area immediately outside the Law Library in the Four Courts (if you live in Dublin) or at any venue suitable to both parties (if you live outside Dublin). Your solicitor will notify you in advance where and when the settlement consultation will take place. They are usually held between 1 pm and 2 pm, or after 4 pm, when the courts are not sitting.

If your case is at the stage where there is a barrister involved, the barrister, in consultation with your solicitor, will discuss with you the merits of your case, and on the basis of the medical reports will advise on the value of the case.

After consulting with you, your legal advisers will negotiate a settlement on your behalf. If an offer is put to you, you are free to accept or reject the offer. Be guided by your legal advisers.

In some settlement negotiations, a range of options may be put to you by your legal advisers. It is advisable to bring along a spouse or a friend to use as a sounding board and for moral support.

Settling a case before going to court is a compromise situation for both sides. The other side may not wish to incur the costs of running the case. You may not wish to undergo the ordeal of going to court and giving evidence.

For both parties, in some instances, going to court can be a risk. If you are made an offer to settle, there is no guarantee if the case were to proceed to trial that you would get more. You may well get more, but you might be awarded less or even lose the case. If the other side offer to settle your case, your solicitor may advise against an early settlement because of the nature of your injuries. Settlement will not be recommended until the medical reports are fairly clear on your prognosis (in other words, what will happen to your injuries in the future – will they clear completely or will you always be troubled by some complication).

Any acceptance of a settlement is final. If your injuries worsen later or complications develop, you cannot claim any further compensation.

ASSESSMENTS
If liability is not an issue in your case (that is, if the other side admit that they are responsible for your injuries), an offer may have been made to settle the case. You and your lawyers may be of the opinion that the amount offered is not enough and that the offer should be refused. If this is the situation, then the matter is set down for trial and all that the judge will be asked to do is to assess the amount of money your case is worth. This

is called an assessment, and the court case will run along the following lines:

- If the medical reports from the two sides are not agreed, then the doctors will be consulted on either side and called to give their medical evidence. They will be examined and cross-examined by your legal advisers and that of the other side;
- when they have finished giving evidence, you will be called on to give an account of your injuries and subsequent treatment and the progress you have made since the accident. Your own barrister will bring you over the facts of your injuries, and the barrister for the other side will cross-examine you in turn;
- at the conclusion of the case, the judge will decide on the award and will give judgment for that amount. The question of costs will depend on whether there was a lodgment in court and whether the award of the judge exceeded the amount lodged.

Remember, assessments only happen when the other side admit liability, and the only matter to be determined is the amount, or quantum, of your award. If this is the case, you will only be required to give evidence about your injuries, treatment and prognosis.

LODGMENT

If an offer is put to you and is rejected, the other side may lodge money in court — an amount which, in their opinion, is the value of your claim. This is called a lodgment.

When your case is heard, the Judge is not told that there is a lodgment in court. If, at the end of the case, the Judge gives an award that is less than the lodgment, you have failed to "beat the lodgment".

If you do not beat the lodgment, you pay not only your own costs from the date the lodgment was made, but also the costs of the other side from the same date. Effectively, you are being penalised for putting the other side to the expense of running the case. In some circumstances, you could end up owing money instead of receiving compensation.

If, however, no offer is made to settle your claim, or if you are advised or decide not to accept an offer, your case proceeds to court. It will be set down for hearing and it will then be allocated a date in court. Your solicitor will notify you when your case is due to be heard.

TAKING AN ACTION

If the other side denies that they were responsible for the accident and your injuries, then it is usual for your solicitor to instruct a barrister to prepare the papers for court action. When your case proceeds to court, it is set down for hearing and will be allocated a date. You will be notified by your solicitor when it is due to be heard.

QUANTUM

Quantum is the amount in money terms which your claim is worth. The court in which your case is heard depends on the value of your case.

The jurisdiction of the courts in respect of personal injury actions is based on the amount of money the different courts are allowed to award. Depending on the value of your claim, your case will be brought in either the District Court, the Circuit Court, or the High Court. The Courts can award the following amounts in respect of compensation in damages for injuries or losses suffered:

- District Court: £1 up to £5,000;
- Circuit Court: £5,000 up to £30,000;
- High Court: Unlimited jurisdiction – any amount in excess of £30,000.

Unlimited jurisdiction means that the High Court can award as much as the court sees fit. Personal injury actions in the High Court usually relate to quite serious injuries.

Your claim is valued by your legal advisers on:

- the nature of your injuries;
- the extent of those injuries;

11

- the prognosis, based on medical reports given by the doctors who treated you.

Valuing a claim is not an exact science. No two claims are ever exactly the same. However, on the basis of your legal advisers' expertise in dealing with such matters, you will be advised on the most appropriate court in which to bring your claim.

PLEADINGS

Pleadings are court documents drawn up by a barrister and are, in effect, a statement of the claim you are making. After you deliver your statement of claim, the other side may ask your solicitor for what are known as particulars.

A request for particulars is a series of questions relating to your claim. In some situations, the other side are entitled to know the answer to these before they decide whether to defend the claim.

The questions asked can relate to your entitlement under the Health Acts — in particular, they may want to know if you are a medical card holder. They may enquire whether you had a previous medical history in respect of the injury you are now complaining of. If you are claiming for medical expenses, they can ask you to provide bills and receipts in respect of these. If you are out of work, you may be asked to state your loss of earnings.

Usually, your solicitor will contact you for the necessary information. It will help if you provide the answers and any documentation speedily and promptly.

THE LEGAL DIARY

Your case will be listed to be heard on the day allocated in the Legal Diary, which contains the listing of all cases in all of the courts on any particular day. Your case will be only one of several cases listed for hearing in a particular court on that day. This is because many cases are settled or adjourned for various reasons before they come for hearing. Despite the number of cases listed for hearing on any single day, a judge may find that there are only a few matters left to deal with. For example, your case may be listed fourth in the Legal Diary for a particular court. If the first case goes on for hearing and the second and third cases settle, then your case follows on after the first case is dealt with.

THE CALL OVER OF THE LIST
At the start of the day, the Court Registrar calls over the list of cases listed for hearing in each court. Your barrister will be in court to inform the judge of the situation in respect of your case. The court will be told whether the case is settled, whether negotiations are in progress or if the case is going on.

THE COURT CASE
At a full hearing (that is, when both liability and quantum must be decided), the case starts when your barrister outlines to the judge what your action is all about. Briefly, the barrister will describe who you are, what you do, your age and how you came to injure yourself.

Then medical evidence will be given by a doctor or specialist. Usually, this evidence is given first to allow them to return to their practices as soon as possible. If your medical reports are agreed by the other side, there will be no need to call medical evidence. An engineer may be called to prove certain matters, such as a map of the accident location or photographs of the scene of the accident.

It is then your turn to give evidence. Your name is called out in court by your barrister, and you go into the witness box. The Court Registrar calls out the oath, phrase by phrase, and you repeat each phrase directly after the Registrar. You will be asked to state your name and then to sit down.

It is very important that you speak clearly and slowly, and loud enough so that both the barrister for the other side and the judge can hear your answers. If you do not hear or understand a question, say so and it will be repeated or rephrased for you.

You will be asked to tell the court how you came to injure yourself. You will be asked to recall, as best you can, your version of the accident. Your injuries and the treatment you received and your progress will be questioned.

After you give your evidence, you will be cross-examined by the barrister for the other side. The object of cross-examination is to suggest to you that, in some respects, your version of events differs from what the witnesses on the other side will say. Their version of events will be explained to you and you will be asked to comment on it.

After your cross-examination, other witnesses for your side will give their evidence and they in turn will be cross-examined by the barrister for the other side. When all the witnesses on your side have given their evidence to the court, that is the end of your side's involvement.

The other side now call their witnesses and they in turn are cross-examined by your barrister.

There is sometimes the possibility that you may be recalled to the witness box to clarify a matter. If you are recalled, there is no need to be sworn again as you are still under oath.

At the end of the other side's evidence, the judge will ask the barristers whether they have anything further to say on the matter. Submissions may be made which will usually refer to points or issues that arose and which either or both sides wish to emphasise further.

Usually, the judge will go through the main issues of the case, and will comment on the evidence produced by both sides. On the basis of the evidence, and of the law as it applies to the circumstances of your case, a decision will be given.

If the judge finds in your favour, the amount of the award will be announced. The award will be made up of an amount for general damages (that is, an award for injury and pain) and an award for special damages (that is, those costs incurred as a result of your accident). Your barrister will also make an application for costs and, usually, this will be granted.

However, if you lose, the barrister for the other side will ask for their costs to be paid. You will be ordered to pay these together with your own costs. In some cases, the judge has a discretion not to penalise the losing side with costs.

As previously explained, the judge may decide that you contributed to the accident in some way. If that is the situation, the judge will reduce your award by a percentage related to your blame. For example, if you were awarded £10,000, to include both your general and special damages, and the judge is of the opinion that you were twenty five percent liable or contributorily negligent, then your award would be reduced to a net award of £7,500.

PAYMENT
When can you expect payment of your award?

Your solicitor should receive a cheque from the other side within four to eight weeks.

Clients sometimes wonder why the cheque is not sent directly to them. As previously explained, your award is a combination of general and special damages. There are some costs which the other side will not pay. These can include consultations you have had with your legal advisers and the costs of medical reports in excess of an agreed amount. These are the solicitor and client costs referred to previously. You will have to visit your solicitor's office to endorse the cheque to enable these bills to be paid.

APPEALING A DECISION
Any party involved in a court case not satisfied with the decision given by the court can appeal the decision to a higher court. For example, if the case commenced in the District Court, it will be appealed to the Circuit Court; if it commenced in the Circuit Court, it will be appealed to the High Court; and if it commenced in the High Court, it will be appealed to the Supreme Court.

Appealing a case means that it is reheard by another judge, in another court, at another time. You will have to go through the entire process again. However, if a case is appealed from the High Court to the Supreme Court, the appeal is heard by way of a transcript of the evidence given in the lower court.

If you lost your case, should you appeal the decision?

This will depend on how the case went, how the evidence unfolded, what stance the judge took on the law as applied to your case, and your own performance as a witness. All of these factors will have to be taken into account. It is a matter for yourself to decide whether you wish to have another bite at the cherry and appeal an adverse decision. Be guided by your legal advisers.

Now look at the other scenario. You have won your case but the other side decides to appeal the decision given in your favour. They can appeal the decision:

- in its entirety: They can argue that the judge was wrong to decide in your favour in the first place;
- on the basis of quantum alone: They can argue that you were awarded too much by the Court.

If a case is appealed in its entirety, a judge hearing the appeal can do one of three things:

- uphold the decision of the original court – that is, you get the same result again;
- overturn the original decision and give the opposite decision;
- increase or decrease the amount of your original award.

If you have been successful in your original action, the other side may decide to appeal to a higher court on the basis of quantum only. They are in effect disputing the amount of your award.

If this is the nature of the appeal, it is more than likely that an alternative offer will be made to you. The offer made will be an amount less than was awarded to you in court. Such an offer is again a compromise situation. You are buying off a risk in agreeing to settle. In return for accepting the offer of the lesser amount, the case will not be appealed. If the case were to be appealed, the original award could be upheld (you still get the same amount), or you could get a lesser amount, in which case you have lost the appeal and you end up paying for the costs of the appeal. There is the possibility, of course, that your award will be increased on appeal. It is up to you on the basis of the advice given to you by your legal advisers whether to accept or reject any such offers made to you, in the full knowledge of the consequences involved in the event of the appeal going ahead.

FATAL ACCIDENTS

The death of a loved one caused by the negligence of another person is a tragedy for all concerned. If a loved one dies in these awful circumstances, the family members affected by the death are entitled to the sum of £7,500, under the terms of the Civil Liability Act. The family members allowed to claim include:

- husband or wife;
- father or mother;
- grandfather or grandmother;
- stepfather or stepmother;
- son or daughter;
- grandson or granddaughter;
- stepson or stepdaughter;
- brother or sister;
- halfbrother or halfsister;
- adopted children.

Where a child is killed, the amount of £7,500 is divided proportionally between all family members concerned. Children who have reached their majority can waive their entitlement in favour of either or both parents if they so wish. In respect of the loss of a child, this amount is all parents and immediate family members are entitled to unless the child contributed to the income of the household.

However, if the deceased had dependents (that is, was married with a wife and family, or if single members of the family were dependent on the deceased's income), actuarial evidence will be given as to the appropriate amount of compensation. To claim compensation, you will have to prove the degree of dependency you had on the deceased.

If a loved one is killed in these circumstances, you must see a solicitor. You will be advised whether, in all the circumstances, you can claim against the other side. Court proceedings will be instituted setting out details of the claim you are making. If agreement is reached with the other side on the appropriate amount, the matter will be brought before the court for ruling. Otherwise, all family members claiming that they were dependent on the deceased will have to come to court to prove their claim.

On the surface, it may appear to be a cold blooded exercise. Nothing is ever going to bring your loved one back to you. You may think it unkind or unfair when you are asked to justify the claim you are making but, as in all claims for compensation, you must be able to prove your claim.

2

NEIGHBOURS

The song that goes with the television series tells us that everybody needs good neighbours. But what happens if relations between you and next door are not so good?

In all disputes between neighbours, the courts try to adopt a policy of "live and let live". In fact, the courts have gone so far as to say that the maintenance of good relations between neighbours is of greater importance than success or failure in legal proceedings.

LIVE AND LET LIVE IN PRACTICE

Neighbours can at times be too close for comfort. However, you do have to get along with them in the long run. At all times, you should be reasonable about any cause of complaint you may have against your neighbours. If possible, state the facts and the nature of your complaint in a reasonable and straightforward manner.

If you engage in any correspondence with your neighbour, do remember to keep copies. Unfortunately, you may need them if the matter ends in court.

Try as best you can not to lose your head. You are going down a very slippery slope if you engage in verbal or physical abuse or if you engage in litigation straight away.

The difficulty with most problems with neighbours is that, unlike other litigation, litigation between neighbours means that you see and hear the other side all day every day. It can be very trying and irritating for all concerned to have to live with the prospect. If dialogue breaks down, you can try perhaps to engage the services of an independent third party — another resident, a mutual friend or even your local friendly Garda

Sergeant, who could perhaps help both parties to agree your differences. If this does not work, then you need a solicitor.

BREACHES OF THE PEACE

The worst possible scenario in most disputes with neighbours is a situation which starts out with verbal abuse and rapidly descends into physical assault. If this is your situation, you may find yourself on the receiving end of a summons to appear in the District Court on breach of the peace charges. The outcome of such a hearing may be that you would be bound over to the peace for a period of time. Any further breaches by you in respect of such an order could result in you being imprisoned.

NUISANCE

In some circumstances, your neighbours' activities and conduct can be a nuisance. This is how the law views unneighbourly conduct.

As the law stands, you are expected to be reasonable about the activities you carry out on your property. Similarly, you must be reasonable about what you can be expected to put up with or accept.

Regardless of the circumstances of the nuisance you allege against your neighbour, in order to have a stateable case in nuisance at law, you must be able to show that as a result of the nuisance there was actual damage caused to your property or there was an interference with your enjoyment of your property, caused by an unreasonable use of the property next door.

REMEDIES

In some situations, you can remedy the breach yourself by removing whatever is causing the nuisance from your own property.

If the situation is sufficiently serious, an application can be made to court for an injunction to prevent or restrain the nuisance continuing or to compel your neighbour to do something that he should do. For example, an injunction could be sought to prevent your neighbour carrying out excavation works to his own property which are causing, or would be likely to cause, subsidence to your adjoining property. An order could also be sought requiring your neighbour to rectify any damage done to your property as a result of his activities.

In the case of unauthorised structures that require planning permission being erected by your neighbour, a complaint can be made to the Enforcement Officer in the Planning Department of your local authority, who will deal with the breach in the interests of good planning and development.

ROOTS AND BRANCHES

What is the situation if roots and branches of trees spread across from your neighbour's property into your own property?

In law, this constitutes a nuisance. In an appropriate case, you may be entitled to seek damages — for example, if the roots encroached into the foundations of your house and caused damage. If no damage has been caused but damage is likely, an application for an injunction may be required. In all situations, your solicitor will advise on the appropriate remedy.

As to remedying the situation yourself, you may cut the roots away as soon as they project onto your property. If branches of trees overhang your property, you are entitled to cut them back. You are also entitled to the fruits of any branches which overhang into your garden or land.

NOISE, VIBRATIONS AND SMELLS

Any complaints about your neighbour's activities which cause noise, vibrations or smells must be supported by evidence that they are seriously interfering with your comfort and enjoyment in your own home.

The case involving the Hanrahan farming family illustrates the point involved. They sued Merck Sharp & Dohme, a nearby chemical plant, on the basis that the escape of noxious or toxic gases from the factory resulted in a deterioration in the family's health. They claimed that their crops and grass did not grow, and their cattle sickened and died. While this was an extreme case, generally speaking the inconvenience and discomfort complained of must be substantial.

COMPETING INTERESTS
There are two sides to every story. In dealing with nuisance matters, the courts will take into account the respective property interests of the parties involved. In most neighbour disputes that come before the courts, compromise on both sides is often the order of the day.

It is not a good idea, no matter how sorely you may be tempted, to fight fire with fire and give your neighbour a taste of his own medicine. If your neighbour plays music which you say is played too long and too loudly, do not retaliate by playing your own hi-fi equally loudly. You may find yourself before the courts to answer your neighbour's charge of nuisance against you.

3

DOGS

Everyone knows that a dog is man's best friend. As the owner of a dog, however, if you fail to control your dog, your best friend can land you in the most terrible trouble. As a dog owner, you are obliged by law to have a licence for your dog. The licence costs £5 and is available from all Post Offices. Failure to have a licence can result in a fine of £100.

THE OBLIGATIONS OF THE OWNER OF A DOG

As the owner of a dog, your main obligation is to control your dog. You are liable for any damage or injury caused by the dog to others. If your dog bites or attacks people or chases cars and bicycles, anybody who crashes or is injured as a result can sue you. Depending on the nature of the attack, an injured party may take an action for personal injuries or damage to property against you. Your first notification of such a course of action will, in all probability, be a solicitor's letter informing you of the fact. If this happens, you should instruct a solicitor to act on your behalf.

To prevent such an awful eventuality occurring, you should not let your dog wander freely about without supervision or control. Unfortunately, even if your dog breaks free without your knowing about it, you are responsible if he causes any injury or damage to anyone else or their property.

Certain breeds of dogs or cross-strains are subject to a recent Ministerial Order, which regulates the appearance of dogs in a public place. The types of dog included in the Order are:

- American Pit Bull Terrier;
- Bull Dog;
- Bull Mastiff;

- Doberman Pincher;
- English Bull Terrier;
- German Shepherd (Alsatian);
- Japanese Akita;
- Japanese Bandog;
- Japanese Tosa;
- Rhodesian Ridgeback;
- Rotweiler;
- Staffordshire Bull Terrier.

You are not allowed to have these dogs out in any public place unless:
- the dog is led by a strong chain or leash, that does not exceed one metre in length;
- the dog is securely muzzled;
- the dog is wearing a collar with the name and address of the owner on a badge or disc;
- the dog is accompanied by a person who is over 16 years of age and is capable of controlling the dog.

If any of these regulations are not complied with, the dog may be seized on the spot by a dog warden. If the dog is believed to be dangerous, the courts have power to order its destruction.

GUARD DOGS
The keeper of a guard dog is held to be strictly liable for any injuries caused to anyone else by a dog trained to attack, if the dog is out of the control of the handler.

If a guard dog is used to protect and guard premises, the guard dog must be accompanied by a handler or secured so that it is unable to roam freely around the premises or escape. A warning notice must be displayed at all entrances to the effect that there is a guard dog on the premises.

The guard dog must wear an identification collar at all times and an electronic device must be implanted under the skin as a permanent means of identification, in the unfortunate event of an attack.

BARKING DOGS

Dogs in urban areas can be a nuisance. The most common cause of complaint is where a dog barks excessively or continuously through the day and night, causing untold annoyance and sleepless nights to families living nearby. How can the law help you in this situation?

As the owner or occupier of property, the law entitles you to enjoy reasonable peace and quiet. If animals are kept in unreasonable numbers or are crying and barking on a continuous basis, they are interfering with this right.

Let us assume you have done all that a reasonable neighbour would be expected to do in the circumstances. You have very politely and repeatedly complained to the neighbours involved. Your complaints have been repeatedly ignored. You are getting nowhere and the dog is still barking away. What can you do?

Any interested person, usually anyone affected by the noise and disturbance, can make a complaint to the District Court. It will cost you £10. You must first serve a notice on the neighbour of your intention to make the complaint.

WHAT CAN THE COURT DO?

The court can order the occupier of the premises in which the dog is kept to stop the nuisance by controlling the dog. If there are a number of dogs on the premises involved, the court can make an order limiting the number of dogs that can be kept on the premises. If the circumstances warrant it, an order may be made to have the dog, or dogs, involved delivered to a dog warden to be destroyed.

DANGEROUS DOGS

Is there a dog in your neighbourhood, which is not only dangerous, but not kept under proper control?

If so, you can make a complaint to the District Court, and the court may order that the dog be properly controlled or destroyed.

FARMERS AND DOGS

The law in relation to farmers and dogs is simple enough. If a farmer finds a dog on his lands and has reason to believe that the dog is or has been worrying sheep, such a belief is a defence if the farmer shoots the dog.

4

FAMILY AFFAIRS

"...........and they all lived happily ever after".

They did, but you did not. The decision to end a marriage, to live your life separate from your partner can be a very difficult decision to make.

There are as many reasons for wanting to end a marriage as there are reasons for deciding to be married in the first place. Your decision to end your marriage may be because of your partner's infidelity, cruelty, meanness or silence. There may be a history of physical violence or an intolerable drink or drug related problem. Maybe, for whatever reason, you are just not getting along any more, and as far as you are concerned the marriage is over.

Family law is a complex area. There are as many remedies available as there are problems. When you do make the decision to do something about your situation, it is vital that you get good legal advice from the start.

If you have money at your disposal, you should make an appointment to visit a solicitor. It is advisable to deal with one who has expertise in dealing with family law matters. A list of solicitors who specialise in this area can be obtained from the Incorporated Law Society on request. Note that if you decide to separate as a couple, you must both instruct separate solicitors, since a solicitor is unable to act for both parties in a dispute. It is better if each spouse gets independent legal advice, rather than relying on their own judgement.

If you do not have access to money, you can apply for Legal Aid (see chapter 17).

SEPARATION
Separations are rarely amicable affairs. Unhappy differences in

a marriage can cause great anxiety and bitterness. It is natural to feel betrayed, bitter, resentful and hurt by the behaviour of the offending spouse. It is a very emotional and traumatic time. Because of what is at stake, it is necessary to be as practical, clear-headed, reasonable and civil as is possible in the circumstances, for your own sake and that of any children.

Before going to a solicitor, be clear in your mind as to why you want to separate. It is not a good idea to use the threat of separation proceedings to force your erring spouse into submission or compliance. It is a waste of your time and effort, as well as money. It can also rebound on you in the worst possible way. You may get what you never really wanted. There are probably other less drastic ways of solving what may be only a rough patch in a marriage. The more appropriate course of action may be marriage guidance or reconciliation, rather than separation.

 ## METHODS OF SEPARATING

There are two methods of separating in Ireland:

- if both partners are in agreement, a Deed of Separation (also known as a separation agreement) can be drawn up by solicitors. Such an arrangement does away with the necessity of going to court;
- in the absence of agreement, either spouse can apply to the court for a Decree of Judicial Separation.

Regardless of which method is used, neither spouse is allowed to remarry. Deeds of Separation and Decrees of Judicial Separation simply end both parties' obligation to live together. Both methods set out to rearrange the affairs of both parties, to take account of a new living situation.

MEDIATION

If both parties in a marriage agree to separate, it can help the separation process if they both engage the services of a trained mediator. A mediator is a trained impartial facilitator, who helps both parties to resolve and rearrange their affairs prior to parting.

The mediation, attended always by both parties, is conducted in a civilised non-contentious atmosphere. It is usual that both spouses have separate independent legal representation, so that anything agreed to in mediation can be referred for approval. This is to safeguard both parties' legal rights. However, nothing agreed to at mediation is legally binding on either party.

It is very important to remember that mediation is not marriage guidance counselling. The aim of the service is not to help parties reconcile but to assist them in the separation process.

SEPARATION AGREEMENTS

Once both parties are in agreement, and both parties' solicitors approve of the terms of the agreement, then a separation agreement is drawn up incorporating the terms and conditions agreed. A separation agreement is a legally binding document that sets out the terms and conditions on which you both will live your future lives, when you become separate.

It is usual to include the following matters in the agreement:
- an agreement to live separate and apart;
- neither spouse to molest or interfere with the other spouse;
- maintenance arrangements for the dependent spouse and children (enforcement and review of such payments may be included);
- custody of the children;
- access to children, together with agreed times and dates for visits at weekends and during school holidays;
- the family home (for example, who has right of residence? how will house contents be divided? if the family home is to be sold, how will the proceeds be divided?);
- inheritance rights (these are usually waived as between the parties).

Separation agreements are legally enforceable agreements from the moment they are signed by both parties.

JUDICIAL SEPARATION

A Decree of Judicial Separation can be granted to an aggrieved spouse in the following circumstances:

- adultery;
- unreasonable behaviour;
- desertion;
- living apart for at least one year, where the other spouse consents to the decree;
- living apart for at least three years, where the other spouse does not consent to the decree;
- breakdown in the normal marital relationship for at least one year.

Even if you satisfy any one of the above conditions, before the court will grant you a decree, the court must be satisfied that:

- you discussed with your solicitor the possibility of reconciliation;
- the solicitor provided you with the names and addresses of trained mediators and marriage guidance councillors;
- the solicitor advised you, if possible, to enter into a Deed of Separation;
- proper provision is made for any children.

If you are granted a Decree of Judicial Separation, the court has power to make additional or ancillary orders to cater for the financial and accommodation needs of the dependent spouse. Depending on your situation, the court can make financial and property orders. These can include:

- the payment of secured periodic payments in respect of maintenance;
- the payment of a lump sum;
- orders relating to the occupation of the family home;
- order for sale of the family home;
- the extinguishing of both spouses' succession rights as regards each other;
- property adjustment orders to achieve a fairer distribution of property.

The aim of these orders is to achieve a fairer distribution of property and assets as between both parties. For example, a Property Transfer Order transfers property from one spouse to the other, for the benefit of the dependent spouse and children. This can be done, regardless of which spouse is the legal owner, or what interest the other spouse has in the property. Depending on individual circumstances, the court may order the sale of the family home and a division of the proceeds of sale. Paramount in the making of any of these orders will be the basic accommodation and financial needs of the dependent spouse and children.

INSTRUCTING A SOLICITOR

Before visiting a solicitor, it is a very good idea to write down the story of your marriage. It helps to clarify matters in your own mind and can be of great assistance to the solicitor in advising on the appropriate course of action.

The points you should cover include:

- **the courtship**: How you met. The attitude of both families. The duration of the engagement. The circumstances of the marriage. Did you have to get married? Was there pressure put on you to get married? The attitude of your partner to the wedding;
- **the marriage**: The date of your marriage and the place where the ceremony took place. The names of your children and their dates of birth (It is very helpful to have copies of your marriage certificate and of your children's birth certificates);
- **the problems**: When, in your opinion, did your marriage start to go wrong? List in chronological order each and every instance of bad or unacceptable behaviour or unpleasant situation. If there was violence involved, were there any witnesses? Did you seek medical help? If infidelity is the problem, say insofar as you can when it first occurred, and when you first discovered it, whether it is continuing and the name of the party or parties involved;

- **the family home**: Describe the circumstances surrounding the purchase of the family home. Who paid the deposit? What contribution (if any) did you make to the deposit and subsequent repayments?
- **finances**: What is the attitude of your spouse to matters of finance? Do you (if you are the wife) get sufficient housekeeping allowances? Are either or both spouses unemployed? If or when you were working, what items of the household budget were you responsible for?

Make a list of all current household expenses because, when you are separated, these will still have to be met:
- mortgage/rent;
- electricty;
- phone;
- fuel;
- car running costs (insurance, tax, petrol, repairs);
- health insurance;
- house and contents insurance;
- groceries;
- school fees/books/uniforms/school trips;
- clothes;
- baby-sitting;
- holidays.

Doing this will help put into perspective the maintenance aspect of the separation.

There are other matters which must be considered. One is the situation in relation to the family home. Another is to decide who is to have custody of the children. The party who gets custody will have to allow the other spouse reasonable access to the children on a regular basis.

THE TAX SITUATION
How you and your spouse will rearrange your tax affairs, once you are separated, will also have to be considered. Married couples who are living separate (whether as a result of a separation agreement, a judicial separation, or a less formal

agreement) are usually taxed as two separate single people, unless they opt for joint assessment.

INDIVIDUAL ASSESSMENT
If both parties opt for this arrangement, they are taxed as separate individuals and receive the appropriate single person's tax allowances.

Maintenance payments made by one spouse for the support of the other spouse are taxed in the hand of the spouse in receipt of maintenance and are allowed as a deduction against income in the hands of the paying spouse. But maintenance payments made in respect of children are *not* subject to any tax in the hands of the spouse in receipt of this element of maintenance.

Each parent is entitled to a single parent's allowance, if they maintain a child at their own expense for part of the tax year. There is a residence requirement which must be observed before both parents can avail of this allowance. It is usually satisfied by allowing the parent who does not have custody to have overnight access or holiday entitlement to the children.

JOINT ASSESSMENT
If both spouses opt for joint assessment, they are taxed as if they are a married couple still living together.

Joint assessment means that both spouses continue to derive all the benefits, reliefs and allowances that are applicable to a married couple. It is of great benefit if there is a substantial mortgage outstanding and where mortgage repayments are being repaid by either or both spouses.

Joint assessment is only available if both spouses are resident in the state for the year of assessment. No allowance is made, or relief available, for the payment of maintenance under this system.

Your solicitor will advise you as to which option is best suited to your own individual circumstances.

GOING TO COURT
After consulting a solicitor, if you find that you do have grounds for a judicial separation, what happens next?

Your solicitor will instruct a barrister who will draw up papers stating your case. These will be served directly on your spouse or on his or her solicitor. It is usual for your spouse's solicitor to reply to the allegations you are making.

The reply may deny or make counter-allegations in respect of your conduct in the marriage.

PSYCHOLOGICAL ASSESSMENTS

If you are claiming custody of the children and the other spouse contests this, the other spouse may insist that the children, together with both parents, are assessed by a child psychologist or psychiatrist. In addition, the Court of its own accord, if the judge thinks it necessary, can appoint a specialist in this area to assess the family.

If a report is necessary, your solicitor will arrange an appointment and you will attend, together with the children. The other spouse will also be seen with the children, though the interviews will be arranged separately. If your spouse wishes to have his or her own psychologist or psychiatrist give a report, you will have to attend and go through the same process again. Reports may then be written by the doctors involved. Recommendations may be made in the reports as to the custody of the children, as well as access arrangements and the conditions for such access.

PRELIMINARY ORDERS

Because of the behaviour of your spouse, it may be necessary for you to apply for a Barring Order, or orders in relation to the custody of the children or protecting the family home and its contents or for maintenance. If the circumstances warrant it, the court will make the necessary order pending the hearing of the matter in full. This is called a Preliminary Order.

THE COURT CASE

When a case is set down for trial by a solicitor, it is given a place in the court list. You have to wait for your case to be reached in the list. Your solicitor will notify you when the case is due to be heard.

As is the case with all court lists, numerous matters are listed for hearing on the same day. Depending on your place in the list, you may have to wait some time before your case is reached. It can sometimes happen that a case which is running does not finish, and your case does not get to go on. In this event, you will be assigned another date for the hearing.

On the day of the case, you will have a pre-trial consultation with your solicitor and the barrister, who will represent you in court, in order to go over certain matters in relation to the case.

There are three points you should note:

- barristers no longer wear wigs and gowns in family law courts;
- all family law matters are heard in camera, which means that only the parties involved and their witnesses are allowed into court.
- witnesses are brought into court one at a time to give their evidence. They leave the court having given their evidence.

THE RUNNING OF THE CASE

At the start of the case, your barrister will briefly outline to the judge what you are asking the court to do. The judge will be told when you were married, the number of children of the marriage, and their ages. The spouse making the application for a judicial separation will be called to give evidence first.

You will be cross-examined by your spouse's barrister. Your spouse will then give evidence and will be cross-examined in turn by your barrister. This only applies to contested matters. If your spouse does not contest the proceedings, then you alone are required to give evidence.

If violence was involved in the course of the marriage, doctors who attended on the aggrieved spouse may also be called to court to give evidence.

If maintenance or custody is in dispute, experts in these areas may be called to give evidence. For example, if one spouse disputes the amount of his or her earnings, his or her accountant may be called to give evidence of income. Similarly, if there is a dispute as to custody of the children, either side may bring evidence before the court from psychiatrists or psychologists as to what party would be best suited to have the care of the children on a permanent basis.

When both sides have given their evidence, the judge may decide the matter there and then. Otherwise, judgment will be reserved to another date and time.

When a decision is given by the judge, an Order as to the costs of the case will also be made. A judge always has a discretion in relation to the payment of costs. The husband may be ordered to pay all the costs on the basis that he is in the best position to do so. If you are legally aided, the Legal Aid Board pays the costs. Sometimes, an order is made to the effect that both sides be responsible for their own costs.

APPEALS
If they do not like the decision made in respect of the case, either party is free to appeal the decision or any part of the decision to a higher court. If they do so, the matter under appeal is reheard in a higher court at another time.

FAILURE TO COMPLY WITH COURT ORDERS
Sometimes the theory of a court order or decision is fine, but the implementation or carrying out of the order can prove to be difficult or impossible. If this is the situation, the offending spouse can be brought before the court to answer why they are in contempt of a court order. If they still refuse to comply, an order for imprisonment can be made.

NULLITY OF MARRIAGE
Depending on the circumstances of your marriage, you may be advised by your solicitor to apply to the High Court for a Decree of Nullity.

A Decree of Nullity declares a marriage to be invalid, on account of some fundamental defect that relates either to the form of the marriage ceremony itself or more usually to the state of mind of either party at the time of the marriage. The effect of a nullity decree is that the marriage is deemed never to have been a valid marriage. Put another way, the decree declares that the marriage never existed.

Nullity is a civil remedy. If you are granted a Decree of Nullity by the court, either party is usually free to remarry in the eyes of the State. However, your religion may not permit remarriage. For example, if you are a Catholic, you are still married in the eyes of the Church, and unless you are granted a Canonical Annulment by the Church (which is an entirely separate process), you are not allowed to remarry in a Catholic church.

THE EFFECT OF A DECREE OF NULLITY ON CHILDREN
The Decree of Nullity effectively puts you back in the single position you were in before you married. The rights of your children of the marriage are protected under the terms of the Status of Children Act, which grants to children born outside marriage much the same rights as children born within marriage. The children's inheritance rights are not interfered with and the father is still obliged to maintain them. The mother is not entitled to maintenance for herself.

If the father is not in a position to pay maintenance for the children, the mother is entitled to Unmarried Mother's Allowance.

Depending on individual circumstances, your solicitor will advise on the situation in your own case as regards property matters.

THE DECREE OF NULLITY
A marriage can be declared to be void or voidable. If a marriage is void, it is said never to have existed in the first place.

The grounds for having a marriage declared void are as follows:
- **the existence of a prior valid marriage**: One party was already married and therefore not free to remarry;
- **at the time of the marriage, either party was under the legal age to marry**: Both parties must have been 16 years of age when the marriage took place;

- **the formalities relating to the marriage ceremony were not observed**: This relates to the rules and regulations laid down in respect of notification of the intention to marry (the publishing of banns); marrying in a church other than the one in which the banns were published; marrying in a Registry Office without notifying the Registrar or without the necessary licence;
- **if it can be proven that, at the time of the marriage ceremony, either party did not freely consent to the marriage by reason of insanity or mental instability, intoxication or duress**: If you are of unsound mind or drunk at the time of the marriage ceremony, you are not in any position to consent freely to what is happening. If either party is pressurised into marrying by fear, threats, intimidation or duress either on the part of the other partner to the marriage or from an independent party, be it parents, or employers, the marriage may be declared to be void, because of the absence of free consent, depending on the particular circumstances of the case;
- **parties are related to each other within the degrees forbidden by law**: By law, a woman may not marry her stepfather, nor may a man marry his son's wife;
- **parties of the same sex**: Even after undergoing a sex-change operation, men who become women may not marry another man.

A marriage which is voidable is valid until it is set aside by the court. A marriage can only be voidable on two grounds:
- **the impotence of either party**: The decree is granted on the inability of a party to the marriage to consummate the marriage;
- **the inability of either party, for whatever reason, to sustain and maintain a normal marital relationship**: The law under this heading is uncertain and the granting of a decree depends on your individual circumstances. The earlier cases in this area were decided primarily on the incapacity of a party to

entertain and sustain the marriage relationship because of mental illness, which existed at the time of the marriage ceremony. This was extended, in some instances, to include emotional instability during the course of the marriage, and some recent cases have involved a high degree of temperamental incompatibility, together with other factors. Your legal advisors will tell you if you have reasonable grounds in this area.

Regardless of whether the decree declares your marriage to be void or voidable, the effect is the same — your marriage no longer exists in the eyes of the State. Like all family matters, nullity applications are heard in camera. Only the parties concerned and their witnesses are allowed into court.

FOREIGN DIVORCES

When, and in what circumstances, are foreign divorces recognised in Ireland?

Central to the whole issue of the recognition of foreign divorces is the concept of domicile. Your domicile is the place where you are permanently resident.

At birth, you automatically acquire the domicile of your father. If born to a single parent, you acquire the domicile of your mother. This is known as a domicile of origin.

Until he or she reaches full age, a child's domicile changes with that of its parents. On reaching full age, a person may acquire a domicile of choice.

If you make the decision to work and live abroad indefinitely, and on a permanent basis, with no intention of returning to your own country, you are said to have abandoned your domicile of origin and adopted the domicile of your country of residence.

Taking out citizenship in another country is usually taken as a sign of change of domicile.

THE DOMICILE AND RECOGNITION OF FOREIGN DIVORCES ACT, 1986

Prior to October 1986, and the passing of this Act, a wife's domicile was based on the domicile of her husband. A wife now has an independent domicile.

A foreign divorce applied for, prior to the 2nd October 1986, is recognised in Ireland if both spouses had their common domicile within the foreign jurisdiction at the date of the institution of the divorce proceedings. So, if both spouses lived and had their domicile in England, and one party applied to the English Courts for a divorce, that divorce is recognised and is valid in Ireland.

The situation since the passing of this Act in October, 1986 is that either spouse can petition the Court for a divorce decree in the country where either is domiciled and, if granted, that divorce will be recognised here, provided that person is domiciled in the country where the decree is obtained.

The mechanics of the recognition of a foreign divorce are now based solely on the domicile of either party; residence is not sufficient. For example, if a couple are married and domiciled in Ireland, and either spouse makes the decision to leave Ireland on a permanent basis, with the intention never to return but instead to start a new life abroad, the spouse who goes abroad can obtain a divorce (if such is available) in the country where he or she is now domiciled.

THE EFFECT OF A VALID DIVORCE

The effects of a validly recognised divorce include:
- if a foreign divorce is validly obtained, both parties are automatically free to remarry in the eyes of the State;
- a wife is not allowed claim maintenance for herself – only for the children;
- a wife loses her own inheritance rights, though those of the children are protected;
- an ex-wife is no longer deemed to be a deserted wife for the purposes of Social Welfare payments, but may be entitled to benefits as an unmarried mother.

41

BARRING ORDERS

A Barring Order is used for the removal of a violent spouse from the family home. It is a remedy that is available to either spouse against the other.

If an application is made to the court for a Barring Order, the court must be satisfied that there is a risk to the safety and welfare of the spouse and children, arising from the serious misconduct of the offending spouse. An isolated act of violence can in some circumstances be sufficient to warrant the granting of a Barring Order if, as a result, the family is living in fear of a repeat episode.

Barring Orders are usually granted where there is a history of violent behaviour. Such behaviour can consist of verbal abuse, the use of foul language or humiliating experiences — in fact, anything that puts the members of a family and spouse in fear and dread.

It can sometimes happen that a spouse is forced to leave the family home and seek shelter or refuge with family or friends. If this is the situation, this spouse can still apply for a Barring Order, removing the other offending spouse from the house, to enable him or her to return to live there with the children.

If you are applying for a judicial separation, the Court can grant an Exclusion Order, as part of the ancillary reliefs. This prevents the offending spouse from living in the family home.

PROTECTION ORDER

As there is usually a time lapse between applying to take out a Barring Order and the court hearing, you can apply to the District Court for a Protection Order, if the circumstances warrant it.

A Protection Order does not exclude the offending spouse from the family home. It orders the offending spouse not to use or threaten to use violence against the other spouse and children, pending the hearing of the Barring Order application.

You can make application yourself for a Protection Order or a Barring Order in any District Court Office. There is no charge for this service. It is usual that a Protection Order would be given immediately by the District Justice, if the circumstances warrant it.

If you have the means you should instruct a solicitor to represent you at the hearing of the Barring Order application. Otherwise you should apply for free legal aid, to your nearest Legal Aid centre (see Part 2 of this book). Regardless of how busy the centres may be on any occasion, provision is always made to deal with emergency applications of this nature. It is not a good idea to represent yourself for such a potentially emotive and fraught application.

THE COURT HEARING
The spouse seeking the Barring Order will be required to give evidence in court in relation to the incidents and degree of violence used. Witnesses may be called — perhaps the family doctor, who treated you for injuries, to give evidence in support of your case. The offending spouse (if he or she is present) will be required to give evidence, and will be subject to cross-examination.

THE EFFECT OF A BARRING ORDER
The consequence of a Barring Order for an offending spouse is very serious. If granted, a Barring Order prevents the spouse from living in the family home for the duration of the order. In some cases, this may be permanent.

Once the Order is made, a copy is sent to both parties as well as to the local Garda Station. If an offending spouse breaches the terms of a Barring Order, he or she can be committed to prison for a period of up to six months and can be fined up to £200.

DURATION OF BARRING ORDER
If application is made to the District Court for a Barring Order, the District Court only has power to bar the offending spouse for a 12 month period. You must reapply if you wish to have the Barring Order renewed at the end of this time.

If, on the other hand, you apply to the Circuit Court, the

Barring Order granted there is usually for an indefinite period, and can be permanent.

GENERAL
It cannot be stressed often enough how vitally important it is to get good advice at an early stage in respect of all family law matters. Because family law issues are so emotionally involved, it can be the most difficult area to be objective about. What you may want and what you get or are entitled to can be very different to your hopes and expectations.

Because separation entails the total rearrangement of your life and perhaps your standard of living, you will have to be prepared, for your own sake and those of any children involved, to put aside as far as possible any feelings of bitterness, hurt and perhaps betrayal. Try to be calm and deal with the situation in a practical business-like and normal manner, as far as is possible in what can be very trying circumstances. Work with your legal advisers, not against them. Remember, they are there to do the very best they can for you in what is probably the worst period of your life.

5

CHILDREN

To keep your child safe and free from harm is every parent's wish. You cannot be with your children all the time and it can happen that they fall into bad company, are led astray, and end up in trouble with the law. They can also be involved in an accident. How does the law deal with children in these circumstances?

CHILDREN IN TROUBLE
It is every parent's worst nightmare – the Garda on the doorstep or on the telephone asks you to come down to the station, because your child has been arrested. The most usual reaction is that there has been some mistake, no child of yours could get into trouble. You arrive at the station and your worst fears are confirmed. There is your child awaiting your arrival. What happens next?

THE JUVENILE LIAISON SYSTEM
The Garda Síochána operate a Juvenile Liaison System, which deals with juvenile offences. Any child between the age of 7 and 18 years is a juvenile for the purpose of the system. The aim of the system is to keep children outside the formal criminal court structure in respect of criminal offences and to deal with the problem at a local level. This is done with the help of Juvenile Liaison Officers, who deal specifically with young offenders and who work with and encourage parents in the management and control of their children. The system operates by administering cautions, together with subsequent supervision of the juvenile offender by the Juvenile Liaison Officer.

CAUTIONS

A caution is not a conviction. Your child will not have a criminal record as a result. On arrival at the station, you will meet your child either in the Public Office area or in a detention room. The nature of the offence committed by your child will be explained to you, in the presence of your child. Generally speaking, in most cases of juvenile crime, children are caught in the act. The child will be asked to admit the offence in your presence. Once your child does this, you will then be free to take him or her home.

If it is your child's first offence, an informal caution will be given by the Juvenile Liaison Officer to the child in your presence. The officer will visit you at home within 28 days to administer the caution. That is usually the end of the matter. If, however, your child is involved in a subsequent offence or a serious matter, a formal caution will be given. If it is decided to administer a formal caution, initially you will be free to take your child home. However, within 28 days, a file on your child will be compiled by the Juvenile Liaison Officer. You and your child will be asked to come down to the station, where the Station Superintendent will administer the formal caution. The child will be supervised for a period of twelve months following a formal caution.

GARDA SUPERVISION

Supervision is divided into two categories:

- **intensive supervision**: This applies to high risk cases, where there is serious crime involved, the juvenile is a persistent offender, or there is a lack of parental support;
- **normal supervision**: This applies to less serious situations. Such supervision takes place on a two to three monthly basis.

There are some offences where the Gardaí do not have a discretion to use the liaison system. In such cases, the file on your child must be sent to the Director of Public Prosecutions

(DPP), who will decide whether to prosecute. Such crimes include:

- aggravated burglary (burglary with violence);
- arson;
- assaults resulting in serious bodily harm;
- buggery;
- dangerous driving, causing death;
- fire arm offences;
- manslaughter;
- murder;
- rape and related offences;
- robbery.

If the DPP decides to prosecute your child, a summons will be served requesting the child to attend at a sitting of the District Juvenile Court. If you do not have the means to pay for legal representation, you are entitled to ask for Legal Aid and the court will appoint a solicitor to represent your child.

CHILDREN IN COURT
Cases in the Children's Court are dealt with in camera. This means no member of the public or press reporters are allowed in court.

Depending on the nature of the offence, the Probation Act may be applied, particularly if it is a first offence. A Judge hearing the case may decide to have your child sent to a special school to be assessed for a three week period to enable the Court to decide what further action, if any, is necessary. A custodial sentence may be given.

CHILDREN AND ACCIDENTS
If your child has been involved in an accident and, as a result, has suffered injuries, what can you do?

On the basis of the information you give on the circumstances of the accident, a solicitor will advise you whether a case can be taken against another party.

Maybe you were not present with your child when the accident occurred. The solicitor may have to undertake enquiries to establish the exact circumstances of events.

TAKING AN ACTION ON A CHILD'S BEHALF
If you are advised by your solicitor that you have a case, you take the action in effect on behalf of your child. Anyone under the age of 18 is an infant or minor in the eyes of the law. Except in very rare circumstances, they cannot sue in their own right or be sued by another party. You are known as the "next friend" of the child.

As with a personal injury action involving adults, your solicitor may have to compile a series of reports in respect of the accident. As the next friend of the child, the costs of the action will be discussed with you and, depending on the nature of the case, the solicitor may require some payment in advance to gather such reports as may be necessary.

Again, as in the case of adults, a letter before action will be sent by the solicitor to the other side asking them to admit liability in respect of the accident.

SETTLEMENT

It could be the case that the other side will accept responsibility in full for the injuries to your child, and will agree to pay compensation. However, unlike an adult settlement, an infant settlement should always be approved or ruled by the court, unless the matter is a very minor one. This is to protect not only the interests of the child but also you and your solicitor from being sued by the child when he or she reaches full age, on the grounds that you did not make the best settlement possible.

This unfortunate situation can arise quite easily. Assume, for example, that your child suffered a fractured leg as a result of the accident. The fracture knits and heals well. An offer is made and accepted on the basis that a full recovery has been made. Twelve months after the settlement has been agreed and accepted, your child starts walking with a limp. Fresh investigation reveals that the injury is much worse than was originally expected and that your child now requires extensive and prolonged orthopaedic treatment with no guarantee of a successful outcome. It is not possible to go back and ask for more compensation, since once a settlement is agreed, it is in full and final satisfaction – otherwise, litigation would be never ending. But your child could later sue you for accepting an inadequate settlement.

By applying to the court to approve the settlement, the interests of the child are protected. Because a child at law cannot speak for himself, the courts must ensure that the child gets the best possible deal and that no unfair advantage is taken of the child. Your views on the offer will be taken into account. If you feel on the basis of sound legal advice that the offer is a good one and should be accepted, you will be asked to swear an affidavit to that effect.

THE RULING OF THE INFANT SETTLEMENT

Your solicitor will notify you when the matter is due to come on in court. Depending on the nature of the child's injuries, it may not be necessary to bring the child along to court. However, if there are scars or other disfigurements remaining, the judge will wish to see the child. Your solicitor will advise you.

If the marks on your child's body are not visible, it is advisable to dress the child in such a manner that clothes are easily removed when the judge views the marks or scars.

On the day of the ruling, you will meet the barrister who will be making the application to the court on the child's behalf. You sit in the body of the court, with the child if you have been told to bring the child along. When the case is called by the court registrar, the barrister will outline the circumstances of the case to the judge. The judge will have read the medical reports prior to the ruling. Usually you will be called to the witness box and sworn in. The judge will ask you questions concerning your child's injuries, the progress the child has made since the accident and your attitude towards the offer being made. If necessary, the judge will see the child. If scars are visible, the judge will look at them in open court. However, if the scars are concealed on the child's body, you will be asked to go into the judge's chambers where the marks can be looked at in private.

Despite the advice given to you to accept the offer, the judge may feel that another or more up-to-date medical report is necessary before the judge will rule and approve the settlement. If this is what is decided, the child will have to be re-examined and the matter put before the court again when the report becomes available. The judge, on the basis of all these opinions, will then decide whether the settlement should be accepted.

If the judge decides that the sum on offer is a good offer, then the settlement will be ruled and an order made that the money be paid into court and invested on behalf of the infant until the infant reaches the age of majority. If there were any medical or other bills incurred as a result of the accident, these amounts will be paid out to your solicitor to enable the solicitor to discharge them. It is usual that a token amount be paid out to the parents in order to buy the child a present as some small compensation for the ordeal.

Sometimes, the amount on offer may seem small on the basis of the injuries which your child suffered. There may however be a problem in relation to liability and you may encounter problems in trying to prove the claim. In this instance, if despite the advice you receive, you still insist on bringing the matter to a full hearing by rejecting the offer made, you run the risk of losing the case.

BEATING THE LODGMENT

The second reason for having an infant settlement ruled by a judge is that if an offer is made and the judge or parents choose to reject it, it is usual for the other side to lodge this amount or another reasonable amount in court. The system of beating the lodgment was explained in relation to personal injuries actions.

The system applies also to children with one major difference. An adult who fails to beat the lodgment in a personal injuries action, has to pay not only their own costs but also those of the other side from the date of lodgment. If an offer is made to an infant and the offer is rejected either by the parents or by the judge who refuses to rule the settlement, the case in the normal course of events goes on for a full hearing. If, at the hearing of the action, the infant is awarded nothing, or an amount less than what was offered and lodged in court, the court has a discretion not to penalise the infant in respect of the costs of the other side.

THE COURT HEARING

What happens if no offer is made, or if an offer is rejected?

The case will go forward for hearing in the normal course. A place will be allocated to it in the court list and you simply wait for your case to be reached. Your solicitor will notify you before the case is due to be heard.

51

You will be expected to attend at court, together with the child, about an hour before the case is due to start. All cases are listed for hearing at the same time. The High Court sits at 11.00 a.m; the Circuit Court at 10.30 a.m.

As explained previously, not every case listed for hearing actually goes on. Some are settled, some are adjourned, and others are not proceeded with, for a variety of reasons. It can be very tiresome hanging around, especially if a young child is involved. Waiting, however, is part of the judicial process and you must be prepared for it when you go to court.

Any case that involves an infant plaintiff is run practically in the same manner as described for adults. The sequence of events follows the same pattern.

CHILDREN GIVING EVIDENCE

What is the situation in relation to your child giving evidence in the witness box?

A lot depends on the age of the child. Generally speaking, it will not be necessary for very young children to give evidence. It is also a matter for your legal advisers as to whether or not your child will be required to give evidence. Age is not a reliable yardstick. Some children are more articulate than others. Some will not remember the details of the accident, due perhaps to the passage of time since it occurred. Again, some children will be frightened of court.

Be guided by your advisers. No one wants to put any child through a traumatic experience or cause any child to be upset. A child can never be forced to take the stand and give evidence in court.

If your child is to give evidence, it is advisable that before coming to court you explain to your child about taking the oath. You must impress upon your child the solemnity of the occasion and the importance of answering truthfully any questions asked.

It is usual at the beginning of the case for the barrister who is representing the child to inform the court that the child will be giving evidence. The judge will probably question the child

52

about the significance of an oath in court. The acceptable reply is that it is a promise to God to tell the truth to the judge in court. This is not a formula but it illustrates in essence what an oath entails.

THE RUNNING OF THE CASE
You, as the parent, may also be called upon during the course of the hearing to give evidence. If you were present when the accident occurred, you will be asked to describe what happened. You may also be asked to give an account of the care the child needed after the accident, or perhaps how in your opinion the child was affected by the accident. For example, if the child was forced to miss school, how this may have affected his development. You will be cross-examined by the barrister for the other side.

The doctors who looked after the child will also be in court to give evidence unless the medical reports have been agreed by the other side.

At the end of the case, the barristers on both sides may address the court.

THE JUDGMENT
In some cases, the judge may wish to rise to consider his decision and judgment may be reserved to another time.

If a decision is given there and then, and the judge finds in favour of the child, the decree awarded will include awards in respect of General and Special damages. In an infant ruling, the bulk of the award will be directed to be lodged and invested on behalf of the child until the child is of full age. Similarly, the expenses incurred on behalf of the child will be ordered to be paid out to the solicitor to be discharged. A small amount may be paid out to the parents in order to treat the child. You will also be given what is known as liberty to apply to the court in respect of the monies invested.

LIBERTY TO APPLY

Liberty to apply means that during the course of the child's minority, that is until the child is eighteen, if circumstances warrant it, the parent or next friend can apply to the Office of the Master of the High Court, which sits at the Four Courts in Dublin, for some sums of money to be paid out on behalf of the child.

You can come in person to the Master's Court, at any time when that court is sitting, or you can apply to the Master by letter, setting out the details and nature of the request. You should also have vouchers or estimates in respect of the matter required by the child. Each application is decided on an individual basis. Again, as with all matters that concern children, the interest and welfare of the child is the paramount consideration of the court. The court will want to ensure that the child benefits and that no money will be used for anything other than what the child needs. If you decide to make the application in person, do remember to bring along any receipts or estimates or indeed a brochure containing details of a school trip (if this is the case). All reasonable requests are usually granted.

What can you apply for?

It is impossible to give instances or a list. As the parent of the child, you are in the best position to know the needs of your child. The most usual applications are in respect of the cost of a school trip abroad or the purchase of a musical instrument that would benefit the child but is beyond the means of the parents.

WARDS OF COURT

In cases of very severe mental or physical disability, or if a very large sum is awarded to a child arising out of a court case, it is more than likely that the child will be made a ward of court. The child is placed under the protection of the court in respect of the award made. If this is the situation, you make any applications for the payment out of any money to the Wards of Court Office, at Áras Uí Dhalaigh, Four Courts, Dublin 7. In very severe cases of injury, such application could be for the

54

cost of a house conversion, or a car specially adapted to the needs of the child.

The request for the paying out of any part of the child's money must be a reasonable one. Money will not be paid out in respect of ordinary running costs incurred on behalf of the normal upkeep and maintenance of the child.

Great care will be taken by the court to ensure that the child is not seen to be given any special privileges as regards other children in the family or neighbourhood.

PAYMENT OUT OF THE AWARD
Once the case is dealt with by the courts, and an award made in the child's favour, the money is lodged in the Accountant's Office of the High Court, where it is invested on behalf of the child.

Large sums of money remain unclaimed and uncollected in the Accountant's Office, simply because parents have perhaps forgotten about the award over the years, or else do not know how to go about claiming the money on behalf of the child. Having gone to the bother of taking an action on behalf of your child, you owe it to them to ensure that they ultimately get their award when they are eighteen.

When your child reaches the age of eighteen, the child becomes legally entitled to the original award together with the accumulated interest. To have the award paid out the child attend at the offices of the Accountant of the High Court in the Four Courts, and bring along a copy of their birth certificate as proof of age. The Accountant will require that the child swear an affidavit, stating:
- who he or she is;
- that there is an award that was made in their favour on a certain date;
- that they are entitled to have the money paid out to them, by virtue of the fact that they are now of full age.

The staff of the Accountant's Office will assist in swearing the affidavit. The money is then paid out and that ends the matter. Parents should remember that the onus is on them to ensure that, when a child reaches eighteen, they ensure that the child takes the necessary steps to recover his or her award.

REACHING MAJORITY DURING A CASE

Due to the nature of some injuries, it can sometimes take a long time for a case to be heard.

A parent may commence a court action on behalf of their child, but when the case comes on for hearing the child has reached his or her majority. In this situation, at the start of the case, the barrister representing your child makes an application for the child to be allowed to proceed in his own name and in his own right. If this occurs, the parent as the "next best friend" will have no further involvement in the case, unless called as a witness.

6

DEATH

Making a will is a task most people put on the long finger. The thought of death is not pleasant, and making a will brings home to us the one certainty in life — death. But not making a will can result in unnecessary hardship for those left behind.

Sometimes, people believe they have little or no wealth to leave when they die. But, often, the truism that you are worth more dead than alive becomes very apparent when it comes to adding up the value of your estate.

When you die, your estate is the total of everything you own less the total of all your debts and liabilities. It includes your house, car, savings or investments, life assurance policy, the capitalised value of your pension or perhaps a lump sum paid by your employer to your dependents on your death.

Not having your affairs in proper order could mean that your dependents would have to pay out large parts of your estate to the Revenue Commissioners in satisfaction of unpaid taxes and interest — and that is before you think about Capital Acquisitions Tax.

CAPITAL ACQUISITIONS TAX
Capital Acquisitions Tax (CAT) is a tax on gifts and inheritances paid by the person who receives the gift or inheritance. It does not apply between spouses.

A child of a deceased person can inherit up to the sum of £156,000, free of CAT. A parent, grandparent, brother, sister, grandchild, niece or nephew can inherit up to £20,800, before becoming liable to pay CAT. Anyone else is free to receive up to £10,400; after that they pay CAT on what they receive.

It is the person who receives the gift or inheritance who is liable to pay CAT. To calculate what is payable, all gifts received during the lifetime of the donor (lifetime gifts) are added to any inheritance they may also have been given; once this figure exceeds the appropriate threshold for the relationship between donor and recipient, CAT becomes payable. Your solicitor will advise on any tax liability.

MAKING A WILL

Making a will is not an expensive business. Solicitors charge a nominal amount for drawing up a standard will.

If you are unwell or unable, for whatever reason, to attend a solicitor's office, most solicitors will agree to meet you at home or in hospital.

If your circumstances change, you can visit your solicitor to make changes or alterations to your original will, or indeed to draw up a new will.

If you have young children, it is vitally important that you make a will. Their future welfare must be provided for if you or your spouse are not able to do so.

Husbands and wives can make individual wills, leaving everything to each other. In the unfortunate event of both dying together, a trust should be set up to provide for the children. In your will, you should name trustees and guardians — that is, people of your choice who would agree to be responsible for the upbringing of your children and who would also deal with their financial welfare, if the need arose.

Elderly parents should consider what is to become of the family home after their death, particularly if there are any family members living in the home with them. The interest of these family members ought to be protected. If there is no will, the family members remaining in the family home could find themselves homeless, because in some circumstances other family members would be entitled to force a sale of the home to get their share of the estate. Because of their age or financial circumstances, those left in the family home may be unable to raise funds sufficient to buy out the share of the other family members. To leave a situation that is dependent on the goodwill of all family members may be unfair on some of them; far better that you make a will now that is fair to all the family.

DYING INTESTATE

If you do not make a will, or if you draw up a home made will that is deemed to be invalid after your death, you are said to have died intestate. Your estate is distributed not according to your wishes but in accordance with the law of intestacy.

In the case of intestacy, if the deceased is:

- **married with no children**: Spouse inherits all;
- **married with children**: Spouse entitled to two thirds; remaining one third divided equally between all children;
- **single parent**: Child or children inherit all;
- **unmarried**: Parents inherit equally; one parent deceased, surviving parent inherits all;
- **both parents deceased**: Estate divided equally between brothers and sisters.

If a brother or sister of the intestate person is also deceased, his or her children receive the deceased parent's portion of the estate.

Having spent a lifetime working to provide a home for your family, some savings and the protection of life assurance, it would be tragic if at the end of your life your wishes were not carried out, simply because you neglected to make a will. You should make a will now to ensure that your family will be provided for and will have no cause to worry in the untimely event of your death.

ADMINISTERING AN ESTATE

The terms *grant of probate* and *letters of administration* refer to the documents you receive once the affairs of the deceased have been dealt with. They entitle the person named to deal with the estate of the deceased.

If there is a valid will, you get a grant of probate.

Letters of administration are granted if the deceased died without having made a will.

It is usual when a will is made that executors are appointed. The solicitor who drew up the will may be named the executor and the estate will be taken care of in that event by the solicitor, jointly with any other executor.

If there is no will in existence, it is usually the person most closely related to the deceased who takes out letters of administration. In the case of a married couple, it is the surviving spouse who would do all that is necessary. In the case of an unmarried person who had no children, the parents would deal with the matter. If the parents were deceased, then the surviving brothers and sisters could decide amongst themselves who would undertake the task.

A person will only be appointed as an executor or administrator of an estate if they are resident in Ireland.

DUTIES OF AN EXECUTOR

If you are named an executor in a will, what are your duties?
They are:
- to bury the deceased;
- to prove the will;
- to collect the estate and, if necessary, to convert it into money;
- to pay any debts due and owing;
- to pay the legacies and distribute the residue.

PERSONAL APPLICATIONS

It is possible, in certain circumstances, to take out a grant of probate or letters of administration yourself but it is not recommended if the estate is complex. Similarly, if there is any problem with the will, the matter is best left to a solicitor to deal with. The Probate Office frequently deals with people who are out of their depth as personal applicants and has dormant files going back years, because the applicants were put off by the work involved.

As a personal applicant, administrator of an estate or executor of a will , your primary duty is to administer the estate of the deceased, either in accordance with the wishes of the deceased (if there is a will), or in accordance with the law as it applies to intestate succession. Where there is no will, as the administrator, you are obliged to see to it that everybody who is entitled to share in the estate does so.

To safeguard against the possibility of someone not administering the estate properly, the administrator is required to have a guarantor or independent surety, who must be worth twice the value of the estate and be resident in Ireland. If, as an administrator, you are unable to find someone who would be willing to act as an independent surety, you must take out an *administration bond*. An *administration bond* is, in effect, insurance against the possibility of an administrator not doing what they are supposed to do. Insurance companies will only give such bonds to a solicitor. Administration bonds will not be given to personal applicants.

The personal application procedure is set out below to give you some idea of what is involved. A solicitor, if acting as administrator or executor, will follow much the same steps in administering an estate.

THE PERSONAL APPLICATION PROCEDURE

If you decide to administer the estate personally, you must first contact the Probate Office in your area. If the deceased died in Dublin, Meath, Kildare, or Wicklow, the Probate Office, located at Áras Uí Dhálaigh, Inns Quay, Dublin 7, will deal with the application.

There are 14 District Probate Registries located in the following places and dealing with the following areas:
- Castlebar: Co. Mayo;
- Cavan: Co. Cavan and Co. Longford;
- Clonmel: Co. Tipperary;
- Cork: Co. Cork;
- Dundalk: Co. Louth and Co. Monaghan;
- Galway: Co. Galway and Co. Roscommon;
- Kilkenny: Co. Kilkenny, Carlow and Laois;
- Lifford: Co. Donegal;
- Limerick: Co. Limerick and Co. Clare;

- Mullingar: Co. Westmeath and Co. Offaly;
- Sligo: Co. Sligo and Co. Leitrim;
- Tralee: Co. Kerry;
- Waterford: Co. Waterford;
- Wexford: Co. Wexford.

WHAT DOES PERSONAL APPLICATION INVOLVE?

You start the personal application process by requesting, by phone or letter, a personal application form from the Probate Office that covers the area where the deceased lived.

The form requires you to fill in the following information relating to the financial affairs of the deceased (if the deceased did not have any of the following, simply state *NONE* on the relevant parts of the form):
- insurance or life assurance policies (the sum payable to the beneficiary must be stated);
- superannuation payments;
- bank balances;
- saving accounts;
- gratuities;
- death benefits;
- prize bonds;
- stock and share certificates;
- the current market value of the house property;
- an estimate of house contents (not the amount for which they are insured but an estimate of their value if sold);
- the current market value of the deceased's car;
- any other assets known to you.

Having listed the assets of the deceased, you now have to list the debts that remain outstanding at the date of death. These will usually include the following:
- funeral expenses;
- the mortgage outstanding;
- taxes due and owing;
- any other debts or loans incurred by the deceased.

Details in relation to money accounts of the deceased are usually easy enough to deal with. You need simply write to the financial institution concerned, addressing your letter to the branch manager and requesting the information for the purposes of administering the estate of the deceased. But how do you go about giving estimates in relation to other property owned by the deceased?

HOUSE PROPERTY
A reasonable valuation is all that is required. If you have no idea as to the value of the house, you could visit a local auctioneer and make enquires on its current market value.

CARS
This value is based on the make, model, and age of the car at the time of death. You can check the current value by looking in the newspapers to see how similar models are priced. If this proves to be of no assistance, the AA or your local garage will give you an estimate.

AGRICULTURAL LAND
If the deceased had agricultural land, occasionally the value of the land may be required to be verified by an auctioneer. An affidavit (a sworn statement) may sometimes be required.

TAXES DUE AND OWING
You may need to visit the deceased's accountant to find out what taxes are due and owing. Depending on how up to date the deceased's tax affairs were at the time of death and their complexity, you may get a good estimate at a first meeting with the accountant. In many cases, however, it may take some time before a tax liability can be agreed with the Revenue Commissioners.

THE PRELIMINARY INTERVIEW
Having completed the form in full, you return it to the appropriate Probate Office. Your application will be acknowledged,

and you will be given an appointment to attend at the office for a preliminary interview.

On the appointed day, take with you to the interview all the documents relating to the affairs of the deceased. If there is a will, this must be produced together with a copy of the death certificate. The official in the Probate Office will go through the documents with you. If any matters need to be clarified or additional information is necessary, he or she will request it.

Part of the official's job is to ensure that the will (if there is one) is valid. This may involve one or more of the witnesses to the will attending the Probate Office for interview.

THE FINAL INTERVIEW
At this interview, you will be given a grant of probate or letters of administration, as appropriate. If there is no will, you will need a guarantor as previously explained. The guarantor must attend with you at the Probate Office for your final interview.

Once you receive the grant of probate or letters of administration, you need only produce the relevant document in order to have any monies released to you. You can ask for certified copies, if you will be dealing with financial institutions, which may each require a copy for their files. You must then distribute the estate, having first converted it into cash, if this is necessary, and paid any debts due and owing.

COSTS
The fee payable to the Probate Office depends on the total value of the estate, and is determined on a sliding scale. At 1 September 1991, it ranged from £12, for an estate valued at £500, up to £240, for an estate valued at £200,000.

TAX AFFIDAVIT
As part of the procedure involved in taking out a personal application for grant of probate, you are obliged to swear an affidavit for the purposes of tax. The Probate Office will assist you with this.

TIDYING UP

A house in joint names is not part of the estate of the deceased. If the house is in joint names, the surviving spouse or owner can arrange to have the property transferred into their own name. If there is still a mortgage outstanding, send a copy of the death certificate to the lender and the deceased's name will simply be deleted from the title record. If, however, the house is in the deceased's sole name, you must visit a solicitor to arrange to have the title deeds transferred into your own name, if you are the beneficiary. If this is not done now, it may cause complications at a later date.

When the deceased's affairs are finally in order, one of the first things you yourself should do, if you have not done so already, is make a will. We are unable to choose the time or manner of our departure from this life. We can however make it easier for our loved ones left behind. Making a will is one of the kindest and most considerate things you can do for your family.

Having made a will do remember to tell someone where it is to be found after your death — remember you will not be around to enlighten them. One way to do this, and to avoid difficulties as to whether there was a later will, is to register your will with the National Register of Wills & Testaments, Ross Business Centre, Ross House, Victoria Place, Galway. It costs £10 and provides an unquestionable record of the date of your will and its contents. You can, of course, update your will at any time and register the updated version with the National Register. You could also leave it with your solicitor or bank.

HOME MADE WILLS

In the interest of all concerned and, in particular, your immediate family, do not make a home made will. Instead of saving legal costs, the greatest beneficiary of this course of action may be the legal profession, as the costs of any litigation concerning the validity of the will come out of the estate.

The rules and regulations in relation to a valid will are complex. There are strict rules in relation to, amongst other

things, witnessing a will. Witnesses of a signature on a will can not inherit or benefit under the will.

Under the Succession Act, you do not have complete freedom to leave your wealth as you like in your will. For example, by law, a spouse in entitled to a minimum of one third of the entire estate if there are children, and half the estate if there are no children (unless, of course, spouses have waived their succession rights as between each other).

Do not do yourself, or any beneficiary, an injustice by attempting to draw up your own will. Visit a solicitor and put your own and your family's minds at rest, before you go to your own rest.

PLANNING

On the stress scale, the death of a spouse rates highest of all. The shock of the loss, the trauma of the funeral, and the feeling of aloneness is a devastating experience. On top of this, the surviving spouse can find him or herself, for the first time ever perhaps, responsible for the organisation of the affairs of the deceased spouse, and the reorganisation of their own personal and financial affairs.

When someone dies their bank and other accounts are frozen, pending what is known as the administration of the estate. If, as a couple, you do not have a joint bank or building society account, you could find yourself in a situation where you do not have any access to money after your spouse in whose name the account is held dies. It is essential that couples have at least one account in joint names.

Second, prepare a note of people to contact, funeral wishes, where important documents are kept, what life assurance cover you have (and how to claim on it), the location and account numbers of bank accounts, a list of investments — all the information that your family and executor will have to find after you die.

Some of this information will change from time to time. You may change jobs, terminate life assurance policies and take out new ones, open and close bank accounts, or change your investment holdings. So you should review your list at least once a year, to bring the information up to date.

Put your note in a safe place and make sure your family know where to find it.

A Personal Facts booklet, into which you put all this information, is published by Oak Tree Press, and is available at most book outlets.

Third, make sure your family is aware of life assurance policies held in trust for them. These do not form part of your estate but claims will need to be made to recover the amounts due. These amounts are payable to the beneficiary named in the policy and, as stated before, do not form part of the estate. They may be subject to CAT in the normal way.

7

LOTTO

Chance would be a fine thing you think, as you fill in your Lotto coupon. It turns out to be very fine indeed — you win. After all, somebody has to win, but this time, it is you — you alone, you and a syndicate, you and a neighbour or friend.

Your dreams are coming true before your very eyes. A new house, a new car, holidays, early retirement, parties, a nest egg and security — it is all possible now.

Except that someone else is claiming a share in your good fortune and instead of going on a spending spree, you are going to the High Court to protect what you say is yours.

"It would never happen to us", you say and your syndicate members nods in agreement, as you read about yet another Lotto dispute in court. What can you do to protect yourself from misunderstanding, bitterness, bad blood, envy and greed?

SYNDICATES

Most syndicates or informal arrangements for the sharing of Lotto rely on friendship or mutual trust. Unfortunately, friendship and trust can be misplaced. Far better for all concerned, to have a formal agreement. That way, everyone knows where they stand and disputes are less likely to occur.

You need to decide on these two key points:
- will prize money be shared equally between all members of the syndicate (and, if not, how will it be shared)?
- will it be a case of if you are not in, you cannot win (or will you make provision for syndicate members who are sick, who forget, or are on holiday)?

By deciding these points now, you can eliminate the source of the main problems that beset informal syndicates of this kind.

AN AGREEMENT
A simple agreement can be put in writing and should be signed by all members of the syndicate. Here is a suggested format:

> *We, the undersigned, agree to be part of a syndicate for playing Lotto.*
> *We agree that all prize money is to be shared equally between ourselves.*

We agree that every member pays the sum of £(insert amount)
once/twice (delete as appropriate) weekly for the purpose of
*   playing Lotto.*
We agree that all money must be paid in advance of any draw
by all members. Each member is individually responsible for
paying in advance. Any member who does not pay in advance
of any draw will not participate in such draw nor will they be
entitled to any share in money won as a result of such draw. In
that event, any prize money will be shared equally between the
remaining fully paid up members.
Signed (all members sign)

Each member should be given a copy of the agreement and the
original kept in a safe place. It may seem unduly legalistic but
better to be safe than sorry.

WHAT HAPPENS IF YOU WIN
Everyone in the syndicate should sign the winning ticket. A
member of the syndicate should be nominated to accept the
cheque on behalf of the syndicate and to divide the winnings
accordingly.

If there is any dispute about a Lotto ticket, or a share in a
ticket, no prize money will be paid out in respect of the matter
disputed until the courts or the parties involved have resolved
the situation.

8

HOLIDAYS

You have saved for it, dreamed of it, looked forward to it, travelled with hope and the expectation of a good time — but the holiday turns out to be a disaster. It can be caused by a single catastrophe or a series of minor irritations, all of which make you arrive home feeling much worse then when you started out.

TRAVEL AGENTS AND TOUR OPERATORS
When you book a holiday, you are entering into a contract. A package holiday is usually booked through a travel agent, whose role is to assist the public in booking and choosing a holiday.

Your holiday contract, however, is with the tour operator — the company that put the holiday package together. The tour operator is obliged by law to check out what is being sold to the consumer by way of a package holiday.

The tour operator has a duty to select competent sub-contractors — that is, people who will provide proper holiday services and facilities, such as airlines, hotels and apartments, transfers between the airport and the resort – and to provide competent representatives on the spot who will be able to deal with any problems that may arise.

COMPLAINTS
When you enter into a holiday contract with the tour operator, you are generally bound by the terms and conditions of the holiday contract, which are printed in the holiday brochure.

Basically, you must do what the contract states you are to do, in the event that you have a cause for complaint against the tour operator. For example, if on arrival at the resort your accommodation turns out to be substandard, remote, dirty, or noisy, under the conditions contained in most holiday contracts, you must make any complaints you may have on the spot to the courier (some contracts insist that you put the complaint in writing). If you do not do this, you have not given the tour operator any opportunity of remedying the situation.

There is usually a further requirement, if you are still dissatisfied, that any such complaint reaches the tour operator within a specified number of days (it varies from tour operator to tour operator) after the end of the holiday.

ARBITRATION

If things go wrong, most holiday contracts usually contain an arbitration clause. This usually states that any complaints about a holiday must be dealt with by means of the arbitration scheme of the Irish Travel Agents' Association. An arbitrator is an independent person usually chosen and agreed to by both sides in a dispute.

Under the ITAA scheme for dealing with disputes, if it is decided that the matter should go to arbitration, both sides are responsible for their own costs under the scheme.

If you choose to deal with the matter yourself under the ITAA scheme, you must write within the time specified in your holiday contract to the tour operator involved setting out details of your complaint. If you do not receive a response from the tour operator within six weeks, or if you are unhappy with the response you do get, you should then write to ITAA, at 32 South William Street, Dublin 2, setting out details of the complaint. If ITAA is unable to resolve the dispute, an arbitrator will be appointed to deal with the matter. Under the scheme, the dispute will be dealt with within two months. At the time of writing, major changes are proposed for the ITAA arbitration scheme.

There is nothing to prevent you from putting the matter in the hands of a solicitor to deal with on your behalf. Similarly, if the company you booked your holiday with is not a member of ITAA, a solicitor will advise you on the best course of action.

HOW TO COMPLAIN

First, find the courier or the tour operator's representative. Then point out, and keep pointing out, the inadequacies of the situation on the spot. Ask to be moved, to a different apartment or hotel or resort, if you think this may resolve the situation.

If you get no response or no adequate response, put your complaint to the courier in writing and keep a copy. Document your surroundings. Take photographs and keep the negatives – a picture paints a thousand words – and they may be useful later.

Misdescriptions and misrepresentations would warrant a complaint to the Director of Consumer Affairs. If the complaint is valid and justified, he will take the appropriate action against the tour operator. As explained previously, you can use the Irish Travel Agents' Association's scheme to complain or put the matter in the hands of a solicitor .

There are as many complaints as there are holidays. What is acceptable to some holiday-makers is not acceptable to others. In a lot of cases, it is a question of degree.

We now turn to the most common problems encountered by holiday-makers.

FLIGHT DELAYS

If your flight is delayed due to bad weather conditions, industrial action, or a technical fault, the tour operator has no control over the situation.

He must do all that a reasonable tour operator would be expected to do in the circumstances. This includes providing proper information on the up to date situation, as well as providing meals and hotel accommodation, if these are necessary because of the length of the delay.

Any money to be provided as compensation in these situations is usually written into the holiday contract as a fixed amount.

OVERBOOKING

If, on arrival at your resort, your accommodation is overbooked, accommodation of a similar standard to that booked must be provided. If the only accommodation available is of a standard superior to the accommodation you booked, you are not obliged to pay the difference.

If, however, the only accommodation available is below the standard of your booking, then reasonable compensation should be paid to you.

INDUSTRIAL ACTION
If details of the industrial action is known to the tour operator prior to your departure, you must be told about it in advance and offered other accommodation or a full refund.

If the industrial action only arises after your departure, the tour operator has no control over the situation. He must do all that a reasonable tour operator would be expected to do in the circumstances. This may include extending your holiday, moving you to another resort, or altering the timing and route of your flight home and notifying you accordingly.

DANGERS AT THE RESORT
The seepage of raw sewage in a leading Spanish resort and the escape of gas in Portuguese apartments some time ago are examples of how things can go badly wrong on holiday, sometimes putting holiday-makers in danger.

If such matters are known to the tour operator before you are due to travel, you must be offered another holiday or a full refund.

If the situation is not discovered until after you arrive in the resort, the courier must do all that a reasonable tour operator would be expected to do in the circumstances. What can be done will very much depend on the situation.

LAGER LOUTS
The arrival of an undesirable element in an apartment block or hotel can ruin a holiday. It is, however, beyond the control of the tour operator. The responsibility to control the situation lies

with the hotel management and the local police.

However, you should inform the tour operator's representative and see if there is any other accommodation available at the resort, if you think the situation reasonably warrants it.

COLLAPSE OF A TOUR OPERATOR

By law, tour operators must be bonded. Bonding means that the tour operator makes an arrangement with an insurance company to insure against the risk of being unable to honour the holiday contracts he entered into. The effect of bonding is that, if a bonded tour operator ceases trading while you are away on a holiday arranged by the tour operator, arrangements will be made either for your holiday to continue as planned or for you to be flown home immediately.

If the tour operator ceases to trade before you travel and you have paid a deposit or the full amount of the holiday, you will be entitled to a full refund. Details of how to claim a refund will usually be published in the newspapers following the collapse of a tour operator.

COMPENSATION

Some holiday contracts have an upper limit of £5,000 which can be paid in respect of compensation.

In a lot of cases, however, you will not be entitled to a refund of the cost of your entire holiday. What you may be complaining about may very well be only a component part of the actual holiday. Even though, to your mind, the bad accommodation ruined the entire holiday, accommodation, while central to your holiday's enjoyment, is not the only element which goes to make up a holiday.

There is also a question of degree to be considered. For example, the tour operator's brochure may describe the beach as only a leisurely stroll away. If on arrival, though, you discover that the beach is a good hour away, you have reasonable grounds for complaint — you would have a less valid complaint if it were a 20 minute walk.

If, however, the sea view promised in the brochure can only be glimpsed on a clear day from the tenth floor balcony, and you are in the basement, or if you paid for a sea view and on arrival at the resort one was not available, any extra money you may have paid for the view must be refunded.

BREACH OF CONTRACT

Failure on the part of the tour operator to do all or any of the things promised in the brochure – particularly those for which you paid extra – leaves the tour operator open to being sued for breach of contract.

When you sue for breach of contract, you are in effect suing for the loss of bargain. You are saying that you did not get what you paid for or what was agreed.

If the holiday you book turns out to be not as described in the brochure, this can constitute an offence under the Consumer Information Act. If a complaint is made to the Director of Consumer Affairs, action may be taken against the tour operator by the Director. However, this is a criminal sanction and, in reporting the matter to the offices of the Director of Consumer Affairs, you will not be entitled to any compensation.

9

THE CONSUMER

You bought a toaster and it will not toast; the washing machine will not wash; the ten rolls of wallpaper you ordered from the sample book turn out to be putrid puce and not blazing burgundy; you bought a tea-set that was sold in a box with a picture on the front showing a blue and white willow pattern but when you take it home and open the box, the set is psychedelic pink with green spots.

What rights do you have as a consumer, if there is something wrong with goods purchased?

A consumer who buys goods or hires goods has several rights against the shopkeeper or hirer under the Sale of Goods and Supply of Services Act of 1980:

- **the goods must be of merchantable quality**: If the product does not do what it is supposed to do, it is not of merchantable quality. So, if the carving knife will not cut, or the heater will not heat, you are entitled to a full refund;

- **the goods must be reasonably fit for their particular purpose**: A step ladder must be capable of bearing the weight of a person using it. Similarly, a lawn mower must be capable of cutting grass;

- **the goods must be the same as their description**: If there is a picture of the item on the box, the contents must be the same inside. The same applies to items described in writing or goods advertised;

- **the goods must conform to the sample shown**: If you buy a carpet or wallpaper from the sample shown to you from a sample book, the actual product must correspond to the sample shown.

ENFORCING YOUR RIGHTS

If the goods are defective, in any way, the retailer is obliged by law to put things right. As a consumer, you are entitled either to a refund or replacement of the defective item.

If the item you purchased is faulty, you must bring it back to the shop as soon as possible. By law, you are entitled to a full refund and you are within your rights to refuse all offers of repairs, replacements or adjustments. By delaying in returning the item, you may lose your right to a refund and may only be entitled to a partial refund. For example, if you have used the item and it breaks down, you may only be entitled to have the item repaired. Similarly, if you alter the goods in some way (for example, by putting new buttons on a blouse or changing the covers on a sofa), your right to a full refund may be lost.

WHEN COMPLAINTS ARE NOT JUSTIFIED

There are some occasions when consumer complaints are not justified. For example:

- if the defect is due to the consumer misusing or abusing the goods, there is no entitlement to claim a refund or replacement item;
- if the retailer specifically pointed out any defect to the consumer before the item was purchased, the consumer cannot complain afterwards;
- if before purchasing the goods, the consumer had examined the goods and had the opportunity of looking for defects which would have been obvious, the consumer cannot afterwards complain to the shop about the defect;
- if the consumer buys goods that are clearly marked substandard or seconds, the consumer is not entitled to complain about any defects, once the goods are purchased;
- if the consumer changes his or her mind about a purchase, they have no right to a refund. Let us assume a woman buys a new dress. She brings it home and her

husband hates it. Under the law, she is not entitled to either a refund or an exchange simply because she has changed her mind.

CREDIT NOTES

If your complaint as a consumer is a valid one, the law entitles you to a full refund of the purchase price of the item in question. You may, if you wish, have a replacement – but this must be your choice, not the shopkeeper's.

If the item is faulty from the start and the retailer will only offer you a credit note, this is not an adequate remedy under the law. If you wish, you may accept a credit note, but you are entitled to a full refund.

GUARANTEES

The Sale of Goods Act does not require the manufacturer of goods to give a guarantee with the product. However, if a written guarantee is given with consumer goods, it must be in accordance with the following rules:

- the guarantee must be clearly legible and must refer to specific goods;
- the name and address of the person offering the guarantee must be clearly stated;
- the period of the guarantee from the date of purchase must be stated;
- how to go about making a complaint must be stated;
- the remedies offered by the guarantor must be stated, whether refund, replacement or repair;
- the costs to be incurred by the purchaser in relation to postage must be stated.

Regardless of the method of purchase, be it on hire purchase or a rental agreement, the same rights apply.

SERVICES

Consumers have rights when they avail of services that turn out to be unsatisfactory. If you engage someone to provide a service – for example, to have clothes dry cleaned, a house repainted, or an antique watch repaired – you are entitled to have the service provided on the following terms:

- that the person supplying the service has the necessary skill to provide the service;
- that skill and diligence will be used in providing the service;
- that any materials used will be sound and fit for whatever purpose is intended;
- that items supplied as part of the service will be of merchantable quality.

Depending on the circumstances of the complaint, the consumer may be entitled to a full refund, a partial refund, or an offer to put things right.

EXCLUSION CLAUSES

If, in a contract for the supply of a service, an exclusion clause is inserted to the effect that *all work carried out is at the owner's risk*, what is the situation?

The exclusion clause is only valid if it is brought to the attention of the consumer, and is reasonable in all the circumstances. For example, the repair of a very delicate piece of china may not be successful, despite all the skill and diligence on the part of the repairer. Provided the repairer pointed this out at the time you placed the item with him for repair, you would have no grounds for complaint if he were unable to repair your piece of china.

MOTORCARS

Apart from buying a house, a car is probably the most expensive purchase made by a consumer. When you buy a car, it must be:

- of merchantable quality;
- reasonably fit for its purpose;
- as described.

In addition, under the Sale of Goods and Supply of Services Act, at the time of delivery of the car in question, the car must be free from any defects which would make it a danger to the new owner or any passenger travelling in it or any other road user.

If you buy a car and it proves to be dangerous, what can you do?

Depending on the circumstances, you may have the right to reject the car and claim a full refund and, in addition, claim damages over and above the cost of the car.

An action for damages must be commenced within two years after you have accepted delivery of the car. However the action must be based on the claim that the defect complained of existed at the time you actually purchased the car.

As the seller of the car, to safeguard yourself from being sued by the buyer, you should have the car you are selling checked out by a mechanic. Any defects or faults will be detected and can be pointed out to a prospective buyer.

If your car is in a dangerous condition and fit only to be sold for scrap or parts, you should *always* inform the purchaser *in writing* that the car is not roadworthy and is sold on that basis.

The above does not apply if you sell your car to a dealer. It is the dealer's responsibility when reselling the car to guarantee that it is not dangerous.

UNSOLICITED GOODS

What is the situation if you are sent items that you neither asked for or ordered?

You should write to the sender and request that the goods be removed, at the sender's expense.

If, after six months and no effort has been made to take the goods back, under the law you are entitled to keep them.

GENERAL

If you encounter difficulties in respect of matters affecting goods and services, contact the Office of the Director of Consumer Affairs (see Chapter 19 for address).

10

MOTOR OFFENCES

DRUNK DRIVING
The law in relation to drunk driving is based on the incapacity
of a driver, due to drink or drugs, to have proper control of a
motor vehicle.

A request to "blow into the bag" can be a sobering experience.
You will be requested to take a breath test, if the Garda is of the
opinion that you are "under the influence of drink (or drugs)".

If after blowing into the bag, the results are not favourable,
you can be arrested without a warrant. You must be told that
you are being arrested and the reason for the arrest. You will be
cautioned that you do not have to say anything but, if you do,
it will be taken down and may be used in evidence against you.

Part of the evidence that may be used against you in court
will be the notes the Garda took of your behaviour. For
example, were your movements coordinated? Was your speech
slurred? Was there a smell of alcohol?

In the station, a doctor will be called. You can, if you like, call
your own doctor, but this will be at your own expense. The
doctor will warn you that you do not have to submit to a
general examination but, if you do, the results may be used in
evidence against you.

BLOOD AND URINE SPECIMENS
You will be asked whether you wish to provide a urine sample.
The alternative is to allow the doctor to take a blood sample.

Two samples of either urine or blood will be taken. You will
be offered one of the samples to keep. The other will be retained
by the Gardaí and will be sent to the medical bureau for
analysis. There, the concentration of alcohol or drugs will be

determined. As soon as practicable, the medical bureau will send the Garda Station a certificate stating the results of the analysis. You will receive a similar certificate.

Failure on your part to provide a sample is an offence, as is a refusal to take the breath test. Penalties for such failure or refusal are a fine of up to £1,000 and/or imprisonment for up to six months. You may also be disqualified from driving for a year.

Normally, you will be kept in the station until you are deemed fit to be released — generally, when you have sobered up, if you have not already sobered up with the fright! You will be released on station bail.

THE COURT HEARING

A summons will duly arrive (if you are found to be over the limit), requiring you to attend at the District Court at a specified time.

You should get legal representation for the hearing – consult a solicitor. Whatever chance you may have of getting off on a technicality, you have none if you represent yourself.

An adverse decision in the District Court can be appealed to the Circuit Court, as a complete rehearing of the case.

At present, the penalties on conviction are a fine of up to £1,000 and twelve months disqualification from driving.

DANGEROUS DRIVING

Under the law, you are not allowed to drive a motor vehicle in a public place in a manner which would be dangerous to the public. Matters which will be taken into account will include:

- the speed limit;
- the type of vehicle you are driving;
- the volume of traffic at the time;
- the nature of the place;
- the weather and lighting conditions at the time.

It is a question of fact in each case as to what constitutes dangerous driving.

The penalty for dangerous driving on conviction is a fine not exceeding £1,000 and/or a term of imprisonment not exceeding six months. Dangerous driving causing death or serious bodily harm to another person can result in a fine not exceeding £3,000 and, on indictment, penal servitude for a term not exceeding five years.

CARELESS DRIVING

A charge of dangerous driving can be reduced to one of careless driving. Careless driving can amount to momentary in-attentiveness or sheer carelessness — for example, indicating right and turning left.

On conviction, you can be fined £300 and/or three months imprisonment. If it is your third offence in three years, your driving licence will be endorsed. An endorsement on a driving licence is a record of a criminal conviction.

If an Order is made against you, you must hand in your licence to the Court Registrar, who within five days of the Order being made will return the licence to you duly endorsed. An endorsement will have an effect on your no claims bonus for insurance purposes.

SPEEDING

Driving in excess of the speed applicable to the area and vehicle is an offence. It is a matter of opinion in each case as to the speed of the vehicle involved. The most usual evidence is the testimony of a Garda who followed you in a car or on a motorcycle. New radar controls are being used by the Gardai, which automatically note the speed of your vehicle. These make the evidence against you more certain.

Speeding is a summary offence and is dealt with in the District Court. A summons will be sent, informing you of the date of the hearing and the Court where the case is to be heard.

For a first offence, you can be fined up to £150. On a second offence, you can be fined up to £350. On a third offence committed within twelve months of a previous offence, you can be fined up to £350 and/or imprisoned for a term of up to three months.

PARKING FINES

Going to court for a parking fine summons is the usual experience most people have of attending court.

When you receive the reminder to pay the fine, if you do not do so within the period specified, you will be served with a summons requiring you to attend at a sitting of the District Court at a time and place specified.

If you do not attend, the matter will be dealt with in your absence. Details of the fine imposed (if any) will be sent to you.

If you choose to attend court to answer to the charge, you must be in court at the time specified in the summons. When your name and case number is called, you stand up. The Judge will turn to the prosecuting Garda or road Traffic Warden and ask for the evidence.

When details of the offence have been given to the Judge, you will be asked whether you wish to say anything. You should simply give the reason a fine should not be imposed. The Judge will either accept or reject the reason given. If the reason is accepted, the case is struck out; if not, a fine is imposed.

If you are dissatisfied with the result, you can appeal the matter to the Circuit Court. The Fines Office will assist you in making any such appeal.

11

PLANNING

Our environment is part of what we are. It is the air we breathe, the sights we see, the emissions we smell, the noises we hear.

The planning authorities — the Corporations, County Councils and Urban District Councils — are by law the protectors of the environment. They are obliged to regulate proper planning and development in the areas for which they are responsible, in the interest of the common good.

PLANNING PERMISSION

Ownership of land does not entitle you to develop your land as you wish. You are obliged by law to apply for planning permission, if you wish to develop or make any material alteration to the property or to change the use of the property (say, from a residential use to a business use). You need planning permission for anything that would have a material effect on the area surrounding your property, or for anything that would materially affect the external appearance of your property.

Planning permission is required for the following:
- building a house;
- building a house extension that exceeds 23 sq. metres in area, including a conservatory;
- erecting signs or changing signs on a business premises;
- erecting or changing a shop front;
- creating or changing an entrance to premises from a public road;
- erecting advertising hoardings;
- extending or changing factory premises;
- changing the use of premises from a house use into separate apartments, or from residential to a business use;

- building or extending a car park.

This list is not exhaustive. If in doubt about any proposed development, check with your local planning authority to see whether planning permission is required.

EXEMPTED DEVELOPMENT
Exempted development is development for which you do not need planning permission. For example, you do not need planning permission for:
- an extension that is less than 23 sq. metres in area;
- any internal works carried out
- the erection of a shed or greenhouse (within the grounds of a house);
- the building of a fence or wall, which must not exceed 2 metres (or if it is a boundary wall or in front of a house, must not exceed 1.2 metres);
- the laying of a path or pond that does not exceed 1 metre above or below the level of the adjoining ground

However, in such cases, the development may need Bye Law approval, depending on where you live (see below).

DEVELOPMENT PLAN
To regulate proper planning and development, planning authorities are obliged to draw up a Development Plan for every area and review the plan every 5 years. The plan, which is on display in the Planning Office in your area, indicates the zoning of land in any particular area.

Land is generally zoned for residential, amenity, commercial or industrial use. Some areas will have a mixed use, that is a combination of types of use permitted. Any proposed plan you have for developing land must be in accordance with the Development Plan for your area. For example, if you have a large plot of land at the bottom of your garden in an area zoned for residential use, it is very unlikely that you would be permitted to develop the land by erecting a factory on the site.

BUILDING WITHOUT PLANNING PERMISSION

What happens if you decide to build a kitchen extension or make other changes to your house, without applying for the necessary planning permission?

Anyone can report your unauthorised extension to the Enforcement Officer of the planning authority in your area. You could be required to demolish the structure or modify it to conform with the requirements of the planning authorities.

You may also be required to apply for retention of a structure, which entails in effect applying for planning permission retrospectively.

If no one makes a complaint, then all is well until you want to sell your home. No lending agency will advance loans for property that contains unauthorised structures or alterations. To sell your property, you may be obliged to demolish the structure or seek retrospective planning permission or try to get an architect's certificate stating that the structure or alteration is in accordance with Bye Law specifications.

Far from adding to the value of your property, an unauthorised structure or alteration can decrease the value of the property and cause problems in putting matters right. You would be well advised to get it right at the beginning.

APPLYING FOR PLANNING PERMISSION

It is usual for the architect, engineer or draughtsman who draws up the plans for your development to make the necessary application to the planning authorities on your behalf. There is a set procedure involved in applying for planning permission.

It is as follows:

- **the newspaper advertisement**: You are required by law to advertise your intention to seek planning permission by putting a notice in a newspaper that circulates in the area where your land is located, or by erecting a notice on the land or structure in question. This is to enable the public at large, and in particular your immediate neighbours, to know what it is you are planning to do.

The advertisement of your intention to apply for planning permission will enable any interested party to participate in the planning process, by objecting to your plans, if they are of the opinion that the development you propose would have an adverse effect on their environment. The planning application must be submitted within 2 weeks of the newspaper notice;

- **the contents of the newspaper notice**: The newspaper notice must contain the following information:
  — the name of the city, county or town where the land is located;
  — the name of the person applying for the planning permission;
  — the address of the site or land must be stated;
  — the nature and extent of the proposed development that you plan to carry out must be stated.

TYPE OF PLANNING PERMISSION
You must decide in advance what type of planning permission you are looking for. There are three types:
- outline permission;
- approval;
- permission.

You need to know the distinction between the three types, and be able to decide which is appropriate for in your situation.

OUTLINE PERMISSION
You apply for outline permission, if you want to "test the water". You may be trying to gauge the reaction of the planning authority to your proposal. Also, you may not want to incur any great expense in having detailed plans drawn up at this stage.

If you submit an application for outline permission and it is granted, it does not mean that you can commence building or carry out your conversion. All it means is that the planning authority has agreed to your development in principle (that is, that they will allow you to build a factory or extend your

kitchen). The next step is for you to have your full plans drawn up and submitted. The plans, which must be submitted for approval, will contain full details of the development.

APPROVAL
If you have applied for outline planning permission and it has been granted, you then apply for approval to the planning authority. Outline permission and approval is, in effect, a two step procedure in applying for planning permission.

PERMISSION
If you have detailed plans already drawn up, you can apply for permission from the outset in a single step procedure. This way, however, if planning permission is refused, your costs in drawing the plans will be wasted.

FILLING IN THE PLANNING APPLICATION FORM
The form for planning application must be completed in full and must include:
- the name and address of the applicant;
- particulars of the interest you have in the land (owner, leaseholder, tenant);
- a copy of the newspaper advertisement or the notice erected on the site;
- plans, drawing and maps to enable the planning authority to properly consider your application. (The level of detail required depends on whether outline or full planning permission is sought);
- the appropriate fee (the amount of the fee is usually printed on the back of the application form).

HOW LONG WILL IT TAKE FOR A DECISION TO BE GIVEN?
The planning authority has two months, from the time they receive a *proper* application, in which to give a decision. However, it can request further details from you or may need to have matters clarified which may delay the process.

DEFAULT PERMISSIONS

If the planning authority does not give you a decision within two months, you are in effect granted planning permission by default. Such default permissions are rare, however, and the two month period can be extended if the planning authority decide they need additional information from you in respect of your proposed plans, before they can make a decision.

DURATION OF PLANNING PERMISSION

If you are granted planning permission, you have 5 years within which to carry out the develpment.

OBJECTIONS

Any person can object to your plans. Any plans you submit are available for inspection by members of the public.

It is most important that any would-be objectors get their objections in to the planning authority as soon as possible. Remember, the planning authority has two months from the date on which the plans are lodged in which to give a decision but it could give a decision in a shorter period. Any objections will be considered by the planning authority and will be taken into consideration in making a decision.

THE DECISION OF THE PLANNING AUTHORITY

The planning authority will notify you of its decision, which will be in one of three forms:
- you may be granted planning permission;
- you may be refused planning permission;
- you may be granted permission, with conditions that will be imposed by the planning authority and indicated on the notice you will receive.

The conditions that a planning authority can impose on your development depend on the nature of the development. The conditions could include changing the entrance to the proposed development, retaining a certain number of trees perhaps, or putting a dormer window in the front of the proposed dwelling rather than in the back (to take into account the objections of residents who are not now overlooked, but would be if your development went ahead in its original format). You must comply with the conditions imposed in order to build your development.

You are not permitted to commence any building until you are in receipt of a grant of planning permission. This will be issued four weeks after you have been notified of the decision.

If, however, you as the applicant or a third party appeal the decision, no works may commence until the matter is determined by an appeal decision from An Bord Pleanála.

What can you do if you are not pleased with the decision of the planning authority? How do you appeal a planning decision?

AN BORD PLEANÁLA
Anyone has the right to appeal a planning decision to Bord Pleanála. The Board acts in effect like the Court of Appeal in respect of planning matters. If an appeal is made to them by any party, the Board rehears the issue in full.

At the end of its enquiry into the matter appealed, the decision of the Board is final. The decision of the Board can be appealed to the High Court, only on a point of law.

APPEALING A PLANNING DECISION
The time limits for making an appeal are strictly enforced. If you do not appeal a planning decision within the time limits specified by Bord Pleanála, you lose your right to appeal.

THE TIME LIMITS
There are two time limits involved for appealing a planning decision to Bord Pleanála. The two time limits depend on who you are and what interest you have in the appeal process:
- if you are appealing a decision given by the planning authority as the applicant (the person who applied for planning permission in the first instance), your appeal must reach Bord Pleanála's offices within one calendar month from the day you actually receive the decision of the planning authority;

- if a third party (an aggrieved neighbour, a Residents' Association who wish to appeal what they see as an adverse decision given by the planning authority, or a person who is simply taking a general interest in the environment) intends to appeal a planning decision to Bord Pleanála, the appeal must be delivered to Bord Pleanála's offices within 21 days from the date the planning authority gave the decision.

If you did not object initially to the planning authority about the development but wish to appeal the planning decision to Bord Pleanála, the onus is on you to find out about the decision. Constant checking with the planning authority is necessary.

LODGING AN APPEAL

Because the time limits are so strict, it is preferable to lodge your appeal by hand if possible. The Board date stamps everything it receives and you will get a receipt on request. If it is not possible to lodge your appeal by hand, it is advisable to send it by registered post. That way you will have proof of posting in the event of any dispute.

Because the time limits are so short, it is acceptable to send a letter to the Board giving notice of your intention to appeal the planning decision given. You must state who you are, what interest you have in the matter, and you should briefly set out the broad grounds of your appeal. You should state that you will forward to the Board more detailed submissions and objections as soon as possible. This letter must be accompanied by the necessary fee payable in respect of the appeal.

THE COSTS OF AN APPEAL

The fee for the applicant is £50 for a non-commercial development and £100 for a commercial planning matter. The fee for a third party is £50, irrespective of the type of development. If, however, an appeal is made by the applicant, the third party may make observations on this appeal for a fee of £15.

If either the applicant or a third party request an oral hearing (most appeals are conducted by correspondence only), an additional fee of £50 must accompany the notice of intention to appeal. The fee for the oral hearing is not refundable in the event of the Board refusing to grant an oral hearing.

If you send in all matters relating to an appeal and omit to include the necessary fee, the Board cannot entertain your appeal and your efforts are wasted.

THE APPEAL PROCESS

What happens after you have submitted your documentation to Bord Pleanála?

The Board should acknowledge receipt of your Appeal within a matter of weeks. The Board will quote you a reference number in respect of the appeal. Make sure that you refer to this number in any correspondence you may have with the Board in the course of the appeal.

The appeal is dealt with through correspondence with all parties concerned. The parties concerned will be the applicant, the planning authority, and in some cases a third party. All parties to an appeal are asked to comment on the other parties' points and arguments in respect of the matter under appeal.

It can happen that the Board may wish to clarify a particular matter or point with you and may request additional information. It is in everybody's interest that any such request is complied with promptly.

REFUSAL TO HOLD AN ORAL HEARING

If any party to an appeal requests an oral hearing and it is refused, the decision of the Board is final. If the Board decides that a matter under appeal can be dealt with by correspondence between the parties, then that is how the appeal will be conducted.

Unlike the planning authorities, Bord Pleanála is not confined to a time limit in giving a decision in respect of a matter under appeal, though there is promise of new legislation to rectify this. Thus, it can be difficult to predict how long the appeal process can take.

In addition, the nature of your appeal may be a complex matter that will require a lot of investigation by the Board's inspectors, or the appeal process could be held up unduly, perhaps due to delay on the part of one or more of the parties to the appeal in responding to a request from the Board for additional information.

When the Board makes a decision in respect of an appeal, it will send all of the parties to the appeal an order, signed and sealed on behalf of the Board, indicating the decision reached. The decision is final. You can only appeal the decision of An Bord Pleanála to the High Court on a point of law.

THE GROUNDS OF APPEAL

We now turn to the recognised and valid grounds which Bord Pleanála can take into account in hearing and determining appeals. You must have a valid reason, *in planning terms*, in order to appeal a decision of a planning authority to Bord Pleanála. It is not sufficient to appeal a decision, simply because you do not personally like the proposed development or because you dislike the applicant. Appeals of this nature are deemed to be of no merit in planning terms.

It is usual for the Board on receipt of an invalid appeal to dismiss it, after giving 7 days notice to the parties of their intention to dismiss the appeal.

The Board is not obliged to wait for you to submit any documentation. The person appealing can forfeit the appeal fee.

It is as well to clarify at this stage the matters which Bord Pleanála is unable to deal with by way of submission. Bord Pleanála can only consider planning matters. It has no powers or functions to deal with other property matters such as trespass, leases, tenancy agreements, boundary disputes, sitting tenants, or rights of way. These matters do affect land and premises but, even if they are part of the dispute, the Board is unable to deal with them. Such matters must be dealt with in a Court of Law.

WHAT CONSTITUTES A PLANNING MATTER?

Depending on the nature of the appeal, the Board will consider some if not all of the following matters:

- the development plan for the area in question will be examined. The zoning for the area will be taken into account and the Board will see if the proposed development fits in with the Development Plan;
- increased traffic or traffic hazards in the area which may be caused by the proposed development;
- the availability of parking;
- the increased noise and dirt that the development would create;
- overlooking, invasion of privacy, blocking of light, creation of shade;
- the proposed development may block out a scenic view thereby destroying the visual amenities of the area;
- the housing density in the area.

Depending on the nature of your appeal, you alone may be in the best position to identify matters that the Board should be made aware of when considering the appeal.

PREPARATION AND PRESENTATION OF AN APPEAL

If at all possible, have your submissions to An Bord Pleanala typed. It is helpful for all concerned if the appeal is presented in the following format:

- state exactly what development you are appealing;
- state the location of the site or building under appeal;
- state the name of the planning authority against whose decision you are appealing;
- state the date on which the planning decision was given;
- state the planning register number on the matter under appeal;
- state your name and address;
- state your interest in the appeal;
- list the grounds of your appeal.

Depending on the nature of the appeal, it may be helpful to

have photographs and sketch maps of the development in question to send with your written submissions.

It can be a useful exercise to check out the planning register for your area to see whether there have been any previous refusals of planning permission in respect of similar types of development in the area. As part of your appeal, you can refer the Board to those previous refusals. Finally, you must state why Bord Pleanála should reverse the decision of the planning authority.

BYE LAW APPROVAL

As explained previously, you need planning permission for any extension you propose to build, if it exceeds 23 sq metres in area. However, if your extension or alteration to your premises internally is less than 23 sq metres, while there is no necessity to apply for planning permission, you must (if you live in certain areas) get the necessary Bye Law approval from the Building Control section of your local authority.

THE NEED FOR BYE LAW APPROVAL

Some local authorities, particularly those in Dublin City and County, Dun Laoghaire and Cork City, are concerned that any extension or alteration you make to your home or property is built to an adequate construction standard.

The primary consideration is to ensure that the proposed structure is a safe one, and that it will not have an adverse effect on people's health and welfare. For example, if you build an extension to your kitchen, you must not build over a main sewer. The possibility of blocking access for maintenance purposes would not only affect you, but your neighbours as well.

Any attic or loft conversion must also conform to a specified ceiling height to ensure that air circulates and that there is adequate ventilation. Additional toilets or shower rooms must have proper plumbing and drainage. Walls, floors and roofs must be structurally adequate.

The need for Bye Law approval is designed to safeguard your investment in your home by ensuring that any building works you plan are carried out properly and to an acceptable standard. The temptation is there, particularly if you are an enthusiastic DIY expert, to go it alone and not bother about getting Bye Law approval. Far from increasing the value of your property, such a course may lead to the situation that when you put your house for sale, no lending institution will advance a loan to a prospective purchaser for your property because of the unauthorised extension or alteration.

Some works, such as garden sheds are exempt from some of the Bye Law regulations, but still must satisfy the Bye Laws relating to open space. There is no such thing as a completely exempted development under Building Bye Laws.

APPLYING FOR BYE LAW APPROVAL

Before you start any work on the proposed extension or alteration, you must apply to the Building Control section of your local authority for the necessary form. This must be completed in full and requires you to state the following:

- the address of the site or house where the proposed works are to be carried out;
- your name and the name of the person or firm who is responsible for preparing the plans you propose to carry out;
- the cubic capacity, floor area and height of the proposed building.

The form must be accompanied by the following:

- two sets of plans for the proposed extension, alterations or conversion;
- two specifications;
- two site location maps;
- the application fee.

The fee in respect of an application for Bye Law approval for a domestic extension/alteration is £30 in Dublin City and County on 1 September 1991. The local authority has two

101

months within which to consider your application. You are not permitted to commence any building works until you get the necessary approval from the authority. If you start building before you get approval, you can be obliged to remove the structure.

Before approval is granted, the local authority may inspect your premises to ascertain whether your drawings/plans are in line with site realities. The plan will be examined and, if the proposal is in accordance with the Bye Laws, a notice of approval will be issued.

When you do get the necessary approval, you must notify the local authority in writing of your intention to commence works. You must also give the local authority notice in writing at least 2 days before you fill in any foundation or cover up any drain, and finally when you have completed the building.

It may seem like a lot of bother to have to go to for what is perhaps a small lean-to or a minor alteration. However, if failing to get the necessary approval ultimately results in your being unable to resell your property, your time, efforts, energy and money on the building works will all have been for nothing. Far from being an addition or improvement to your home, it could amount to a liability.

SELLING YOUR IMPROVED PROPERTY

When you are selling property, you must satisfy the buyer's solicitor that you have the necessary planning permission and Bye Law approval for any extensions or alterations to your property.

If the development has been built since 1970, you will generally need a recognised architect's certificate in a standard format confirming that the development has been carried out in accordance with planning permission/Bye Law approval, or that it is an exempt development and does not require planning permission (though there is no exempt development under Bye Law regulations).

It is a good idea to get the appropriate architect's certificate at the time the work is carried out, as it can be expensive to obtain it at a later date.

Where work has been carried out without the necessary Bye Law approval, it is not possible to get approval from the local authority retrospectively. However, many lending institutions will accept a certificate from an architect stating that the unauthorised work does in fact comply substantially with the Bye Laws. The form of this certificate is agreed between the Royal Institute of the Architects of Ireland and the Incorporated Law Society. Depending on the state of the extension or alteration, an architect may require you to carry out certain remedial works before signing the certificate.

BREACHES OF PLANNING CONTROL

A situation can sometimes arise where a neighbour starts building or carrying out demolition works without having obtained the necessary planning permission, or has been refused planning permission but nonetheless starts work. What can you do if either of these situations occur?

Under the Planning Code, any person can apply to the High Court under Section 27 of the Planning Code for an injunction restraining and preventing the continuance of any breach of the Planning Code. It is important to remember that you do not need to have any particular interest in the lands or premises involved. It has to be said that such applications are expensive and, in most cases, would be beyond the means of many people.

An alternative is to bring the matter to the attention of the planning authority involved. They will inspect the development in question and can take other types of action against the developer involved. The most usual is the issuing and serving on the developer of a Warning Notice, to the effect that if the development continues as it is, the developer will be liable for substantial fines for breach of the Planning Code.

12

BUYING & SELLING A HOUSE

Buying a house is probably the biggest investment most people make in their lifetime. The legal process by which you buy or sell a house is called Conveyancing. Conveyancing can be a very complex and difficult area of law. This chapter is simply a very basic outline of the steps involved in buying and selling property. Your solicitor will ensure in the conveyancing process that you get what you are paying for — a good title to the property involved.

BUYING A HOUSE
When buying a house you will have to budget for the following:
- the deposit for the house (usually 10% of the purchase price);
- the cost of repairs or remedial work to the property;
- professional surveyors fees — for inspecting the property;
- the lending institution's fees and outlays;
- stamp duty (if applicable);
- legal costs and outlay.

PROVISIONAL LOAN APPROVAL
If you are thinking of buying a house, you should apply to a lending institution for provisional loan approval. That way, if you do see a house you will know that funds will be available to you, if all is well with the property you have in mind.

PRIVATE TREATY SALES

There are two ways of buying a house — by private treaty or at an auction.

If you are buying a house by private treaty, you will be dealing with the vendor (the seller) personally or with an estate agent who is acting on the vendor's behalf. Regardless of who you deal with, you should never make a final offer until you have had the property structurally examined by an expert, usually a Chartered Surveyor, Architect, or Engineer.

Be absolutely sure what is involved in the sale. Get a list (preferably in writing) as to what fixtures and fittings are involved. A fixture is something that is permanently attached to the property. Fittings such as carpets and curtains are generally not included in the purchase price unless specifically stated as being included. If you wish to purchase them you may have to negotiate over and above the purchase price.

AUCTIONS

Properties to be sold by auction are usually advertised some three to four weeks before the auction is held. This is to enable any prospective purchasers to have an expert's report done on the property and to enable their lending institution to approve a loan. Your solicitor will also have to check that the title to the property is satisfactory, prior to the auction.

VISITING A SOLICITOR

When you make the decision to buy a house, whether it is by private treaty or by auction, you must visit a solicitor.

A booking deposit may be required. They are not binding on either party. Any booking deposit should be sent by your solicitor.

FORMAL LOAN APPROVAL

Regardless of whether you are buying by private treaty or at auction, the next step is for you to approach the lending institution involved for formal loan approval.

The lending institution will have the property valued. If the valuation is satisfactory and you meet the institution's lending criteria, you will be issued with a formal loan approval.

When you accept the institution's offer of the loan, you must fill in and return the acceptance form (in some cases with a fee) and ensure that your solicitor has a copy of the loan approval in order to make the necessary arrangements to finalise the mortgage on your behalf.

WHAT HAPPENS AT AN AUCTION?

Before deciding to bid for a property at an auction, you must have loan approval from your lending institution and your solicitor must check out the title to the property being auctioned.

On the day of the auction, you can bid yourself or have another person bid on your behalf. This other person can be your solicitor. You should always have a ceiling figure beyond which you cannot go — stick to it.

A reserve is the price below which the property will not be sold. When the property reaches its reserve, the auctioneer will formally notify the bidders that the property is now "on the market". Bidding will continue until the highest bid is accepted. If yours is the highest bid, you sign the contract there and then, and you give a deposit (usually 10% of the purchase price) to the vendor's solicitor. You will be given in exchange a copy of the Contract of Sale to pass on to your own solicitor.

If a property fails to reach its reserve, it will be withdrawn from the auction and the auctioneer will negotiate with the highest bidder. If this fails to sell the house, it will usually be offered for sale by private treaty with a quoted price.

SALE BY PRIVATE TREATY

If you are buying a house by Private Treaty, the closing date for any house purchase is usually 5 weeks from signing contracts unless a different date has been agreed.

Your solicitor will check thoroughly the title to the property you wish to purchase. Your solicitor will ask you to come into the office to sign the contract and it is at this stage you bring with you the 10% deposit of the purchase price.

JOINT OWNERSHIP

When you are signing the contract you must decide in whose name to take the property.

If you are buying on your own, there is no problem.

If, however, you are buying with a spouse it is usual for the property to be put into joint names. This ensures that the surviving spouse automatically inherits the property. Your solicitor will advise you in the circumstances of your case.

REQUISITIONS ON TITLE

When the contract is signed, your solicitor will send it to the vendor's solicitors. Once the contract is accepted by the vendor's solicitor, your own solicitor raises more formal and detailed queries on the title.

There are over 20 pages of questions relating to house purchases. They relate to, among other things, rights of way, services to the property, planning permission or bye law approval, if there are any structures on the premises which require such permission.

When your solicitor is satisfied with the replies to the requisitions, a deed will be drafted by your solicitor transferring the title of the property to you. Your solicitor will also liaise with the lending institution involved to be able to give them the appropriate Certificate of Title.

It is essential for good title that there are no outstanding mortgages or interests affecting the property you are buying. Your solicitor will organise searches in the judgement, bankruptcy and deed offices. If all is not well, you may have to wait until the vendor remedies the problem.

THE CLOSING

When all is in order, the sale can be closed. This is the term for handing over the balance of the purchase money in return for the title deeds and the keys. You will need to arrange house insurance before the closing.

It is usual for you to attend at the solicitor's office in order to sign the documents. The final balance due must be by bank draft or loan cheque payable to your own solicitor or the vendor's solicitor. A personal cheque is not acceptable.

In addition, your solicitor will need a bank draft if there is stamp duty payable on the property. The amount payable depends on the value of the house (a table of the amounts payable is given at the end of this chapter).

You will also need to have a cheque to cover your solicitor's own costs and outlays.

FEES AND OUTLAYS

The final fees payable by you to your solicitor will depend on the title and the work involved. Buyers should budget for 1.5% of the purchase price for a purchase and mortgage. If the purchase price is low and extensive work is required, fees may be based on an item-by-item basis. In any event, you should be aware of the approximate cost before signing the contract. Professional fees are subject to 21% VAT.

Additional outlays vary, but comprise some or all of the following:

- Land Registry (approx)
  - searches £50 ;
  - Commissioners' Fees £10.50;
  - Land Registry (Maximum) £200;
  - copy Folio and Map £9.00;
  - stamp duty on mortgage: 1% of mortgage amount.
- Registry of Deeds (approx)
  - searches £50 – 70;
  - Commissioners' Fees £10.50;
  - stamp duty on mortgage: 1% of mortgage amount;
  - Memorials (to register the deed and mortgage) £42.00.

STAMPING

Your solicitor will submit your title for stamping by the Revenue Commissioners. This occurs if stamp duty has to be paid on the house you have purchased.

Following stamping, the deed is lodged for registration with either the Land Registry or Registry of Deeds depending on the title. The deeds will then be sent to the lending institution involved which will retain them for the duration of the mortgage.

FIRST TIME BUYERS

If you are a first time buyer of a new house or flat which comes within specified size limits (a floor area of less than 1346 sq. ft), you are entitled to a New House Grant of £2,000, provided the house was built by a registered builder. The house must be occupied as your normal place of residence.

Application forms for the grant are available from the Department of the Environment, Ballina, Co. Mayo. The form should be completed and returned as soon as possible after signing contracts. The Department will issue a provisional approval and pay the final grant when they are notified and have confirmed that the house is completed and occupied.

BUYING AN APARTMENT OR TOWN HOUSE

If you buy an apartment, you will usually be given a long lease for the particular apartment. When the development is complete, the builder/owner will transfer the freehold of the common areas to a Management Company. Each apartment owner will be a shareholder in the Management Company, which will be responsible for collecting service charges and paying for insurance and common services.

Many apartment blocks and town houses are private developments which will never be taken over by the local authority, so the owners use a management company to maintain the common areas, roads and services in the complex.

If you are buying a secondhand apartment or town house with a management structure, your solicitor will check how it is run, by whom, and whether there is a contingency fund for major repairs. The contingency fund is used to smooth the cost of major repairs over several years. You could be unlucky and move into an apartment just before major repairs become necessary, after several years of neglect and low service

109

charges. Accounts may also be sought from the management company before your solicitor approves title.

BUYING A NEW HOUSE

When buying a new house, you might also be asked to sign a building agreement, governing the building of the house by reference to specifications which are either given directly to you by the builder or sent with the contract for the sale of the house.

The building agreement provides that the builder will make good any major defects which arise within a period of 18 months after the completion date, and make good any minor defects which arise within the period of 6 months. The following items are normally excluded:

- cracks in plasterwork;
- defects or damage in paintwork or decoration;
- normal shrinkage or expansion of timber;
- damage caused by the operation of any central heating system;
- damage caused by fair wear and tear.

In addition, most new properties are covered by the National Housebuilding Guarantee Scheme, which covers serious structural defects for a period of 6 years following the issue of the Certificate of Guarantee.

SELLING A HOUSE

When selling your house, you have the option of selling it by private treaty or by auction. Be guided by professional advisors as to which type of sale is best for your property. Regardless of which method, you use you must notify your solicitor of your intention to sell and let the solicitor have the title documents.

If there is an existing mortgage, your solicitor will need a signed authorisation from you to be able to take up the title deeds from the lending institution in order to prepare a contract for sale. As this can take up to two weeks, it is important to notify your solicitor as soon as possible, especially in the case of a sale by auction.

PREPARING CONTRACTS

When your solicitor is in receipt of the title deeds, a contract of sale will be drawn up.

If you are selling by auction, the contract details as to the purchaser and purchase price will be blank, pending the sale. Solicitors for prospective buyers will want to check the title deeds and contract conditions before the auction.

If you are selling by private treaty, the contracts will contain full details of the sale including the name of the purchaser, the purchase price and the closing date. The contract will also include any special conditions that you agree with the buyer.

PLANNING

Before finalising contracts for sale of your house your solicitor will need to be satisfied that planning documents are in order. Your solicitor will require planning permission and bye law approval for the house if built since 1st October 1964. In most cases your solicitor will require an architect's certificate confirming compliance with the conditions in the planning permission and bye law approval. This certificate was probably given to your solicitor at time of purchase and will be with the title deeds.

Where you have developed the property (and this includes alterations, extensions, conversions or change of use) since 1st October 1964 your solicitor will again require the planning permission and bye law approval with an architect's certificate confirming compliance with the conditions.

If you have carried out a relevant development which was exempt from planning permission it will again be necessary to have an architect's certificate confirming this. It may be that the works are exempt from planning permission but required bye law approval. As it is not possible to obtain retrospective bye law approval an architect's certificate confirming that the works have been carried out in substantial compliance with the bye laws is generally accepted.

If you or the previous owner carried out developments since 1st October 1964 and failed to obtain planning permission or bye law approval it may be necessary to apply for retention permission.

As planning is now a major part of any investigation of title, it is extremely important to have the documentation in order when preparing contracts. If the planning documents are not correct, the Purchaser might not be able to raise the loan and may have to withdraw from the sale.

THE FAMILY HOME

Under the law, a spouse cannot sell or mortgage the family home without the consent of the other spouse. If both spouses are the registered owners, there is no difficulty as both will have to sign the contract and mortgage. However, if only one spouse is the registered owner, the other spouse will have to sign his or her consent on the contracts or mortgage before the sale can proceed.

If the couple are separated, the prospective buyer will require evidence that the separated spouse has no further interest in the property. If there are any difficulties in respect of this area, your solicitor will advise you.

If you are married, you and your spouse will be required to sign a Family Home Protection Act declaration on completion of the sale. You will also have to produce a copy of your State Marriage Certificate. A church certificate is not sufficient.

SIGNING CONTRACTS

Your solicitor will send contracts to the buyer's solicitor for signing, with a copy of the title. The buyer's solicitor will investigate the title and then ask the buyer to call to sign the contract and pay a deposit. Once signed, the contract is returned to your own solicitor. On receipt of the contracts and deposit, your solicitor will ask you (and your spouse if applicable) to call to sign the contract. Any special conditions inserted by the buyer's solicitor will be discussed with you to ensure that they are reasonable and acceptable to you. You will then sign the contracts in duplicate and one part is returned to the buyer's solicitor.

The buyer's solicitor will raise objections and requisitions on title which will have to be answered by your solicitor. If satisfied with the replies, the buyer's solicitor drafts a deed transferring the property to the buyer. In the meantime, your solicitor will prepare the documents for closing and obtain redemption figures for your mortgage from your lending institution.

Before completion of the sale, you and your spouse will need to call and sign the closing documents and declaration.

On the closing date, your solicitor will need keys to the property. There is generally no need for you to attend the closing of the sale. Your solicitor will meet the buyer's solicitor and exchange the title deeds and keys for the purchase money.

Following completion, your solicitor will discharge your mortgage and obtain a formal release from the lending institution. This is then sent to the buyer's solicitor to be retained with the title deeds.

If you obtained bridging funds from a lending institution to purchase another house (pending sale of your own house), your solicitor will send the net proceeds of the sale of your house to your lending institution. The net proceeds are the selling price of your house, less the mortgage, legal and auctioneering fees. At this stage, your solicitor can prepare a final account for you and, if there are no bridging facilities, send you the net proceeds of the sale.

BUYING AND SELLING

It often happens when selling a house that you buy a house at the same time. This can be a stressful time until you are certain that you have binding contracts for both your own sale and your purchase. Follow your solicitor's advice as to the correct procedure.

It is generally advisable to have a binding contract for the purchase of your new house. If you are under pressure to sign contracts for the purchase, these can be signed subject perhaps to a binding contract to sell your own house by a certain date. If the house is not sold by that time, you are entitled to a refund of your deposit and the purchase is at an end.

It may not always be possible, or indeed desirable to try to close both your sale of your old home and purchase of your new home on the same date. This depends on the co-operation of everyone involved in both the sale and the purchase. If there is any unforseen delay, your properly laid plans can fall to pieces.

BRIDGING FINANCE

If you are buying and selling at the same time, you should consider the option of buying your new house some days before completing the sale of your old house. This will involve bridging finance (that is, an application to your lending institution to bridge the gap for funds between the time of paying for your own house and obtaining funds from your own sale).

The lending institution will require confirmation that you have a binding contract to sell your house and a formal undertaking from your solicitor to forward the net proceeds from that sale. As both the purchase and sale will be "up and running" at this stage, this type of bridging will be for a very short period and the net cost should be low. Your solicitor can advise you as to what is best for you at the time of signing contracts.

If you decide to opt for bridging finance, make your application as soon as possible to avoid delays near the closing date.

BUYING, SELLING AND TAX

The most relevant taxes for buying and selling property are Capital Acquisitions Tax and Capital Gains Tax.

Capital Acquisition Tax arises when you sell property which you received as a gift or an inheritance within the past 12 years. In that case, the purchaser will require a certificate from the Revenue Commissioners confirming that this property is free from the tax. This may be with the title deeds; if not, your solicitor will make the appropriate application.

114

Capital Gains Tax arises on sale of property which is not your main residence. If you are selling such a house you should seek your solicitor's advice as to whether you are liable for Capital Gains Tax and the amount payable.

Whether or not a property is your main residence, your solicitor will require a Capital Gains Tax certificate for the purchaser if the purchase price is over £100,000. Again, your solicitor will make application for this certificate and will ask you to sign the appropriate form at the time of signing contracts. Your solicitor will also require your RSI number and Tax District to make the application.

Under present legislation mortgage interest (and bridging interest in certain circumstances) limited to a maximum of £1,600 per person (£3,200 for a married couple) can be offset against income tax. You will be given the appropriate Certificate on completion of your Mortgage to enable you apply for tax relief.

In addition 25% of premiums on all Life Policies (including Endowment Policies) can be offset against income tax subject to a maximum of £250 for a single person and £500 for a married couple. The Assurance Company will issue the appropriate Certificate for forwarding to your Inspector of Taxes.

BUILDING YOUR OWN HOME
Before building your own home, it is essential to obtain proper legal advice.

You will first have to purchase a site, or, if the site is on family land, have it transferred to your own name. It may be necessary to reserve rights of way for access and services to the proposed new house.

Before entering into any agreement to build a property, you will require planning permission and bye law approval if applicable. You will then have to decide whether to employ a contractor, in which case your solicitor may draw up a Building Agreement or build your house by direct labour.

If you plan to borrow part of the cost of the house, you should check the requirements of the lending institution involved.

Your solicitor can then advise as to the correct procedure to ensure that you have a satisfactory agreement with your builder or sub-contractors and a satisfactory title to give a legal mortgage to your lending institution.

STAMP DUTY
Up to £20,000 — 3%
£20,000 – £50,000 — 4%
£50,000 – £60,000 — 5%
£60,000 + — 6%

13

GOING TO COURT

Going to court can be a traumatic experience. It is not a course of action to be taken lightly. Coupled with the fear of the unknown is the fear of losing.

Going to court can be a risk. No matter how good you think your case is, there are always two sides to every story. Everyone feels that their own case is unique and special and is sufficiently important to warrant going to court.

The very thought of having to go to court can invoke feelings of fear and dread, but equally a sense of importance. You have survived the ordeal of your accident, you have been advised and consulted, examined by specialists, and now the time has come to tell your tale.

The fear of speaking in public is a very common one. The thought of going into court and speaking in public about your ordeal can be nerve-racking. The courts, except in family law matters and other sensitive issues, always hear cases in public. How best then can you prepare yourself for going to court?

ON THE DAY
On the day, leave yourself plenty of time to get to the court. If you have any queries, questions or worries, ask your legal advisers' advice.

If at all possible, do have someone come along with you. It helps to have someone to chat to, to pass the time when you are waiting to go into court, and to use as a sounding board if a last minute offer of settlement is made.

Do not under any circumstances bring children along to court — unless they are the injured party. Your mind should be free to concentrate on your case. Do arrange well in advance to have someone look after them for the day.

It is not advisable either to bring an "entourage" along for moral support. Such crowds are frowned upon and they will only be in the way.

You are not allowed to smoke in court or in the corridors and the areas around the court building. It may help to have some sweets handy in case your throat feels dry.

When you are called to give evidence, remember to speak normally but loud enough to be heard. In some courts where there are no microphones, you may be asked to speak up by the Judge. Don't be alarmed, this is quite normal. It can sometimes be difficult to catch everything that is being said in court.

However, you must not sit in the front two rows of court, as these are usually reserved for legal advisers.

Litigants sometimes wonder how they should address the judge, if questioned by the judge directly. In this situation it is quite acceptable to answer the question without calling the judge anything at all.

DRESSING FOR COURT

There are two things you must keep in mind when deciding what you are going to wear for court.

First, if you are the plaintiff, depending on the nature of your injuries, you may have to show the scar or the mark (if there is one) left on your body to the other side and to the Judge. The clothes you wear should take this into account and be of a kind that are easily removable, for your own convenience and to spare you any embarrassment. For example, if you are a girl complaining of scarring on the back of your legs, it would make things easier for all concerned if you wore a skirt and pop socks rather than tight jeans or leggings. If you have facial scars as a result of your injury, you should not attempt to cover them up with make-up. They should be seen exactly as they are.

Second, going to Court is a serious matter. You want to make the right impression. You should, however, feel comfortable. Some people go out and buy a new outfit for the occasion; others go to the other extreme and slip into their most casual gear.

The easiest guideline is to dress for court as if you were going for a job interview. If you dress cleanly, neatly and smartly, you will be fine. If you look right, you will feel right and it will be one less thing for you to worry about.

It is advisable for men to wear a jacket and tie and never to go to the witness box without wearing the jacket.

THE REALITY OF COURT

Subconsciously, people's expectations of court are influenced by court room dramas on television. The reality of an Irish court and its immediate environs can come as a shock.

On television, each episode usually revolves around one case. Clients are seen to get total and undivided attention from their team of legal advisers. Consultations are held in luxurious and well appointed private rooms located near the actual court-room. Hands are held and shoulders patted consolingly, tears are dried and the judge is sitting waiting in expectation of this one and only case to be heard. The case flows without a stutter, stammer or pause on anybody's part. This is not for real.

The reality of court in Ireland, with a few notable exceptions, can be very different. Your case is not the only case that ever was or ever will be. Your place in the court list on the day is shared with countless others. Depending on your place in the list, or on how the other cases fare, you can find yourself waiting around for a considerable period of time before your case is heard. Due to space constraints in the court buildings, you will find that your most private and intimate business is conducted in corridors and crowded hallways in full view of all and sundry. You may be asked to reveal scars and markings and perhaps you may feel that your legal or medical advisers are being brusque or short with you. You may feel that they are not interested in your case as you see it or indeed as you tell it.

You have to realise that what may be of major importance to you in relation to your case may have no value or merit from a legal point of view. Ideally, these matters should have been sorted out before the case reaches court; if, however, you have any fears real or imagined, never be afraid to ask and keep asking until you are satisfied.

It is only natural, given what is at stake, that you may feel vulnerable, out of your depth, afraid of the unknown or intimidated by your surroundings. It may be little consolation to know that every other litigant will feel the same way. As with most ordeals, the anticipation is often worse than the actual event. Knowing as you do now what to expect and what it is all about, you have less to worry about and can concentrate on doing the very best you can on the day.

14

WITNESSES

SUBPOENA TO ATTEND COURT

What happens if you are called as a witness in a court case? You will receive a document called a subpoena (from the Latin, under penalty). You must attend the court on the day appointed; if you do not, you will be in contempt of court and may be fined and/or imprisoned.

A viaticum — a small amount of money, perhaps £5 or £10, paid to enable you to pay your travelling expenses in order to attend court – must accompany the subpoena.

If you are served with what is known as a subpoena duces tecum (from the Latin, under penalty to bring with you), you will be obliged not only to come along to court but to bring with you the documents specified and named in the subpoena.

Reasonable witnesses' expenses are usually allowed to cover the cost of your attendance.

THE HEARING

On the day of the court hearing, you will usually be asked to attend some time before the case is due to be heard. The solicitor and barrister involved on the side which has called you as a witness will question you as to your involvement in the matter.

It can sometimes happen that the other side will have subpoenaed you to attend at the hearing also and, in that instance, you will also be obliged to discuss the matter with them.

When the case goes on in court, at some stage of the proceedings you will be called to give evidence. You will be sworn in and will be examined. You will be cross-examined by the other side. That signals your end in the proceedings, though you should not leave court until the case has finished and the judge has given a decision. There is always a possibility that you may be recalled to clarify a matter.

If either side decides to appeal an adverse decision, you may have to attend again when the appeal is listed for hearing at a later date.

15

JURY SERVICE

A summons has arrived asking you to attend for Jury Service. As a juror, you will be fulfilling one of the oldest functions in the judicial system, that of trying your fellow man. Anyone over the age of eighteen and under seventy years of age, who is on the current electoral register, is obliged to serve on a jury, if called upon to do so.

EXCUSABLE PERSONS

There are categories of people who are not obliged to attend for jury service. If you fall into any of these categories, you may be excused from jury service. These categories are listed on the summons.

You are excused from jury service if you are deemed to be:
- ineligible;
- disqualified;
- excusable as of right;
- you show to the County Registrar's satisfaction that there is a good reason you should be excused.

We will deal with the individual categories separately.

You are ineligible to serve on a jury, if you are concerned in any way with the administration of justice. This category includes practising barristers and solicitors, members of the Gardaí and the defence forces, and personnel working in a Government department who are actively involved with matters of justice or the courts.

You are also ineligible, if you are incapable of serving on a jury. This category is concerned with people who are physically or mentally ill, those who are in hospital or who are obliged to attend hospital on a regular basis, and those who are suffering from any disability which would prevent them from serving on a jury — for example, those who are blind, deaf or dumb, or who are illiterate.

Those disqualified from ever serving on a jury are those who have been convicted of a serious offence in Ireland and who have been sentenced to a term of imprisonment.

Persons excusable as of right include those who provide essential or important services to the community. Into this category come doctors, nurses, dentists, midwives, vets and chemists.

If you are aged between sixty-five and seventy, you are deemed to be excusable as of right, if you do not wish to serve on a jury.

If you are a teacher or a full time student, you may be excused, if the principal or head of your department states that your services are necessary and cannot be reasonably performed by anyone else while you attend for service on a jury.

If you served on a jury before, generally you are not obliged to serve again for another three years. If a jury summons arrives within the three year period, you are excused. Similarly, if you have ever sat on a jury when the judge at the end of the case instructed the jurors that they were exempt from jury service for a period of time (which may have been forever), you are excused.

Even if you do not fall into any of these categories, you may still be excused if you have a valid reason for not attending and this reason is accepted by the County Registrar.

REPLY TO SUMMONS
You must reply to the jury summons. A prepaid envelope is provided.

If you fall into any of the categories excusable from jury service, you must state on the form the category you come into. If you wish for any other reason to be excused, you have to state the reason you wish to be excused. It is then up to the County Registrar to decide if you may be excused.

The summons will tell you when you are obliged to attend for jury service, and where you must attend. Bear in mind that you may never be required to sit on a jury. It will all depend on the number of cases that are due to be tried at any particular time. Other factors can be the availability of judges to hear cases, or the availability of courts.

THE FIRST DAY
You must attend on the first day when the panel is formed, unless otherwise directed. When you arrive in court, the names of all jurors who are obliged to attend will be called out. You must answer when your name is called.

The Registrar will call the cases which require a jury and, depending on the number of cases due to be heard, a jury or a number of juries will be empanelled. The selection of jurors is by ballot. Names are drawn out of a box.

If your name is called, you make your way into the jury box, together with the other jurors selected by ballot. The judge presiding will tell the jurors that, if they are ineligible or disqualified for any reason from serving on a jury, they must say so. If you know the parties or any of the witnesses in the case you will be trying, you must also let the court know.

When the Registrar calls on you to take the oath, you may be challenged by one of the legal teams from the case you are being empanelled to try. This is not a personal slight. An objection to a juror can be made for various reasons and is not a matter you need to concern yourself personally with at all. If you are challenged, you simply return to the body of the court and may get to serve on another jury at a later stage.

Each juror repeats the oath after the Registrar.

The judge can direct that the remaining jurors be released for a period of time. Depending on circumstances, your services may not be required until the following day or for the next couple of days. When you return, the same procedure is gone through again. Do bear in mind that just because you have been called for jury service, it does not automatically mean that you will ever get to serve on an actual jury. You may find yourself hanging around the courts, for the duration of the period you are obliged to attend, without ever being called upon to serve as a juror.

All unsworn jurors are usually discharged until the next day, once the juries for the day have been selected. The selection procedure usually takes about an hour. You may never get to serve on a jury for the duration of your jury service, but you are still obliged to attend until your services are dispensed with by the court.

THE JURY'S FUNCTION IN COURT

Before the case starts, the jury must select a foreman from among its members. The foreman of the jury is the spokesperson for the jury for the duration of the trial. All communications between the judge and the jury are undertaken through the foreman.

In any jury trial, the judge sits in court, aided and assisted by the jury. It is a very important function and obligation to sit on a jury. The judge directs the proceedings and ensures that the correct procedures are followed while the case is being heard. The judge deals with the legal issues in a case; the jury with the facts of the case. In any case, the judge can issue directions to the jury and the jury must follow any such direction.

If you are called on to try a criminal case, after the jury is empanelled, the accused is given into the charge of the jury. The jury is told the nature of the offence with which the accused is charged, and that the jury must decide on the innocence or guilt on the accused on the basis of the facts of the case and the nature of the evidence.

The primary functions of any juror are to listen and observe all that is presented in court and, on the basis of all that you see and hear and the guidelines given by the judge, together with your fellow jurors, to reach a decision on the guilt or innocence of the accused.

THE CONDUCT OF A JURY TRIAL

The case is run along the following lines:

- the case will start with the prosecuting barrister outlining to the jury the facts of the case. The jury will be told how the prosecution intend to prove their case. Members of any jury need have no fear that they will be unable to understand the language or the terminology used by barristers in the course of the trial. The facts will be explained in plain ordinary language. Indeed, the barrister would not be doing a proper job if the jury were unable to understand what was being said;
- the witnesses to help prove the case for the prosecution will then be called to give evidence. Documents or statements may be produced, or exhibits may be used – for example, any dangerous instruments alleged to have been used or forensic evidence. These are usually shown and passed around amongst the jury for their inspection;
- the witnesses are then cross examined by the barrister representing the accused. The defence team representing the accused may, for whatever reason, decide not to call any evidence of their own. There is no obligation on any accused person to give evidence in the course of the trial, since it is for the prosecution to prove the guilt of the accused beyond reasonable doubt. The defence may instead call witnesses who will testify to the character of the accused person.

In any trial, at any stage of the proceedings, the following can occur:

- the judge may, for any reason, withdraw the case from the jury. If this occurs, then that is the end of the matter and the jury is discharged. You are only discharged from that particular trial and you may find yourself sitting hearing another case that is lined up and ready to go on;
- a question of law may arise. As previously explained, any questions of law are of no concern to a jury. You

will be asked by the judge to leave the court while counsel engages in legal argument with the judge. While this "trial within a trial" occurs, the jury may be "out" for a considerable period of time, depending on the complexity of the issue. Jurors are allocated a special room beside the court. You are not allowed to leave the room while the court is hearing legal argument. However, the judge may dispense with your services for the rest of the day and you will be obliged to reattend the following day to continue with the case.

At the end of the case, the jury is addressed by counsel for the prosecution and the defence. They will each give a clear and concise summary of the case. Each side will highlight the merits of their own case. Basically, they will go over the points that the jury will have to keep in mind when reaching their decision.

SUMMING UP
The judge will then charge the jury. This is basically a summing up of the entire case. The purpose of the judge's charge to the jury is to help the jury understand what it is they are expected to do in respect of the case they are trying. You will be told that you must confine yourself to the evidence that has been presented in court. You have to disregard anything you may have read or heard in the media about the case, particularly if the case is one that has attracted considerable media attention. The judge will explain to the jury, that before convicting, the jury must be satisfied of the guilt of the accused beyond reasonable doubt.

BEYOND A REASONABLE DOUBT
Every judge's explanation as to what constitutes reasonable doubt will be expressed in different terms, but the meaning will be the same.

Beyond reasonable doubt means that if there are two reasons given in the case, and both are possible explanations, taken together with the evidence presented, the jury should give the accused the benefit of the doubt. The judge will invariably give examples to the jury to help clarify what is involved.

The actual offence for which the accused is standing trial will be gone into in detail by the judge. The judge will tell the jury what goes to make up the elements of the offence, from a legal point of view. An issue paper will be given to the jury. This simply states the issues that the jury has to consider in relation to the case. The jury may be allowed to take into the jury room any statements made by the accused or any exhibits produced during the course of the trial.

THE JURY VERDICT
Majority verdicts are allowed in criminal trials. On a jury of twelve, if ten members of the jury are in agreement, then that verdict is acceptable. However, in the event of a majority verdict, the jury must have considered the matter for a period of time, which cannot be less than two hours. The jury can come back into court at any time for assistance from the judge.

When the jury has reached a verdict, the jury goes back into court. The Charge Sheet is handed to the Court Registrar, who in turn hands it to the judge. The verdict is then read out in court. That signals the end of your involvement as a juror in that particular matter. You have done the job you have been asked to do. It is usual for the judge to thank the members of the jury for their assistance.

Depending on the nature of the case you have had to try or perhaps the length of time involved, the judge may direct that the jurors are not obliged to serve on another jury for a period of time – perhaps ever again.

If you are called to serve as a juror on a criminal trial, you and your fellow jurors will be provided free of charge with lunch and any other refreshments. Similarly, if the situation warrants it, you may be provided with overnight accommodation, although this is an unlikely event.

However, if you are sitting as a juror in a civil matter, you provide your own lunch and any other refreshments you may require.

16

THE LEGAL SYSTEM

What is the Law? Where does it originate? How is it administered? Who administers it?

On the surface, they appear to be the most basic of questions, yet most people would have some difficulties in answering them.

THE SOURCES OF LAW
There are four main sources of law in Ireland:
- the Constitution; ✗
- the Acts of the Oireachtas; ✗
- the Common Law; ✗
- EC Law. ✗

THE CONSTITUTION
The Constitution of 1937 is the supreme source of law in Ireland. The Constitution provides for the organs of State — that is, how the Country is to be governed.

Central to this is the concept of the separation of powers. Under the Constitution, the ruling of the country is divided into three separate and distinct categories:
- the Executive (government);
- the Legislature (the law making function of government);
- the Judiciary.

As the primary source of law, the Constitution also contains the basic rights of the individual. It contains statements of national beliefs, ideals and aspirations. For example, there is a series of personal rights afforded to every individual in the State, among

131

them the right to free speech, the right to privacy, and the right to ownership of private property.

There is recognition of the family as being the primary and fundamental institution of Irish society. The Constitution guarantees to protect the interest of the family and the institutions of marriage. Any purported interference with these rights must be agreed by the people, hence the recent referenda on divorce and on the right to life.

THE EXECUTIVE

The Executive is the carrying out of government in accordance with the Law. It includes the framing of policy and the manner and means by which effect is to be given to government policy.

The Constitution provides for the appointment of a Taoiseach and fourteen other members of government. The Head of State is the President.

THE LEGISLATURE

The legislative side of government is charged with making laws for the State.

The process of law making is involved and complicated. There is a five stage process, which all bills must go through before being passed into law. The proposer of any Bill is authorised to send a copy of the Bill to all members of the Dáil. This is followed by a general debate, which is followed in turn by a detailed examination of the Bill, clause by clause. This detailed examination is usually done at the Committee stage. Another general debate then follows and, if the Bill is accepted by the Dáil, it is presented to the President to be signed into law.

Under Article 26 of the Constitution, the President has power, after consultation with the Council of State, to refer any Bill to the Supreme Court to consider whether the Bill, or any part of it, is unconstitutional. If the President does this, the Bill is argued in the Supreme Court and, if the Supreme Court decides that the Bill is unconstitutional, the President may not sign it. If a Bill is deemed constitutional, it can never be challenged by any litigant again.

A Bill becomes law on the day on which it is signed by the President, except where a Minsiterial Order is required to bring it into efect.

THE JUDICIARY
The Constitution provides for the appointment of judges to administer the Law. They are appointed by the Government on the advice of the Attorney General.

Article 34 of the Constitution provides for a Court structure. There is a three tiered system:
- an appellate jurisdiction, the Supreme Court, which is a court of final appeal;
- the High Court;
- courts of local and limited jurisdiction — the Circuit Court and District Courts.

THE COMMON LAW
The Common Law is law made by judges. In applying the law and deciding cases, judges rely on earlier decisions given by other judges in respect of similar matters. The judges are aided by the fact that such decisions are written down and are available in the form of Law Reports.

The Common Law system means that there is a tendency to consistency and equality in the application of law in certain areas, which in turn means that there is certainty in the outcome of some matters.

THE LAW OF THE EUROPEAN COMMUNITY
By a referendum held in 1972, the people of Ireland voted to join the EC. This meant that customs barriers between member states would be removed so that there would be free movement of goods, services, workers and professions as between the member states.

EC Law is now part of Irish Law. The Court of Justice of the European Community is the final court of appeal in relation to legal matters concerning Community affairs.

133

In implementing Community Law, the EC uses the following mechanisms:

- **Regulations**: These usually refer to agricultural prices. Once agreed to by the Council of Ministers, they become law in the various member states;
- **Directives**: This method is used to achieve harmony of laws in member states. It allows member states a flexible approach in implementing EC Law, to take into account national situations.

THE COURT STRUCTURE

The Courts in Ireland are as follows:
- the Supreme Court;
- the Court Of Criminal Appeal;
- the High Court;
- the Special Criminal Court;
- the Circuit Court;
- the District Court.

The District Court, the Circuit Court and the High Court have what is known as criminal and civil jurisdiction. The criminal jurisdiction of the various courts is determined by the severity of the crime involved. The civil jurisdiction of the courts refers to the amount in money terms which the various courts can award in respect of damages for breach of contract or for personal injuries.

The Supreme Court and the Court of Criminal Appeal operate only as appeal courts.

THE DISTRICT COURT

In criminal matters, the District Court has what is known as summary jurisdiction. This usually refers to minor offences that carry light punishment (usually a prison sentence of twelve months and a maximum fine of £1,000).

In criminal matters, the District Court sits without a jury. On a preliminary hearing of a matter before the District Court, if the Judge is of the opinion that the case constitutes a minor offence, and if the accused is informed of the right to elect to go forward for a jury trial to the Circuit Court, and if the accused does not object to being tried in the District Court, the judge can hear the case. In some cases, the consent of the Director of Public Prosecutions is also required.

In civil matters, the District Court has power to award up to £5,000 in respect of damages for breach of contract or personal injuries.

PROPOSED SMALL CLAIMS COURT

Under proposed new legislation, the Minister for Justice may introduce a small claims procedure. Initially, the procedure will be available on a pilot basis in the Dublin Metropolitan Courts, in Cork and two other District Court venues. If the pilot scheme proves to be successful, the facility will be extended to all District Court venues.

A claim may be made in the Small Claims Court if it:
- does not exceed £500;
- it is not related to personal injuries, damage arising from a traffic accident, or hire purchase, leasing or other loan arrangements.

It is envisaged that the Small Claims Court would be used in respect of disputes concerning defective goods, or bad or shoddy workmanship.

To make a claim, you will make an application on the appropriate form to the Small Claims Registrar at the nearest District Court Office. A fee of £5 will be payable with each application.

The Small Claims Registrar will consider each application, record the facts and attempt to settle the claim between the parties. If this fails, the matter will be referred to a hearing of the District Court. Each side will be liable for their own witnesses and legal costs (if any are incurred).

THE CIRCUIT COURT

In criminal matters, the Circuit Court deals with indictable offences. These are cases in which the accused is entitled to have his case heard by a judge and jury.

In civil matters, the jurisdiction of the Circuit Court is between £5,000 to £30,000, in respect of damages for personal injuries or breach of contract.

In property matters, the Circuit Court can deal with cases, where the rateable valuation does not exceed £200. Anything in excess of this amount must be heard in the High Court.

THE HIGH COURT

The High Court, when dealing with criminal matters, is known as the Central Criminal Court. It deals with very serious matters such as murder, rape, and treason. When dealing with criminal matters, it sits with a judge and jury.

In civil matters, the High Court has unlimited jurisdiction. It is not constrained or confined in the amounts of money it can award, above £30,000.

THE SUPREME COURT

The Supreme Court is a court of appeal. Matters coming before it on appeal are dealt with from a transcript of the case as it was heard in the lower court. The Court comprises five judges, if dealing with constitutional matters; otherwise, three judges usually sit.

THE COURT OF CRIMINAL APPEAL

This court, like the Supreme Court, has appellate jurisdiction. It always sits with three judges and deals with criminal matters. Those convicted in lower courts can appeal against their conviction and/or sentencing in respect of a decision given in the Circuit Criminal Court, the Central Criminal Court or the Special Criminal Court.

THE SPECIAL CRIMINAL COURT

This court was established for the trial of offences where it is decided that the ordinary courts are not adequate to deal with the matter. It consists of three judges and no jury. It usually deals with situations that involve matters relating to the Offences against the State Act.

JURIES

Juries are no longer required to sit in the High Court to determine awards in respect of compensation for personal injuries. Juries only sit in the High Court in civil matters, in respect of libel and defamation actions and common assault.

In criminal matters, juries sit in the Circuit Criminal Court and the Central Criminal Court.

Your obligations as a juror are set out in the chapter entitled Jury Service.

THE LEGAL PROFESSION

The legal profession is divided into two branches — solicitors and barristers. While both operate separately, their functions are complementary.

SOLICITORS

Solicitors deal directly with the public and are usually the first port of call in respect of any legal problems.

Solicitors take instructions from clients, carry out investigations into the background and the circumstances of cases, obtain reports, give preliminary opinions, and if the matter is one that necessitates a specialist's opinion, or a matter that entails litigation, may instruct a barrister also known as Counsel.

All conveyancing matters (that is, the transfer of property) must be dealt with by solicitors.

Solicitors are allowed to practice as sole practitioners or as part of a partnership in a firm of solicitors.

They have right of audience in all courts in Ireland and may, if they so wish, conduct their own advocacy on behalf of their clients (that is, they may argue a case in court).

BARRISTERS

Barristers, also known as Counsel, are members of the Bar of Ireland. When called to the Bar, a barrister holds himself out as being willing to appear in court, to give legal advice and services for reward. They usually practice from the Law

Library in the Four Courts in Dublin.

Barristers have a right of audience in every court in Ireland.

Barristers do not have direct access to the public and must take instructions in legal matters from solicitors. An exception to this rule is that members of certain professional bodies on the Register of the Bar Council may obtain legal advice from members of the Bar in respect of non-contentious matters.

In court, barristers wear wigs, black gowns and white bands in place of a tie. Solicitors are also entitled to wear a black gown in court, if they so wish.

When called to the Bar, a barrister is entitled to practice law and is known as a Junior Counsel. After a time in practice, a barrister because of sufficient experience or expertise in a particular area may apply to become a Senior Counsel. When a barrister "takes silk" (becomes a Senior Counsel), they are usually no longer concerned with drafting court documents; instead, they give advice and conduct cases.

The term "taking silk" refers to the fact that a Senior Counsel's gown is of a different design to that of Junior Counsel and is made from silk or poplin instead of ordinary cloth.

CHAPTER 17

LEGAL AID

Depending on your circumstances, in respect of a family law matter, you may be entitled to Legal Aid.

ENTITLEMENT TO LEGAL AID

Entitlement to Legal Aid is assessed on the basis of a means test. Basically, you are eligible for Legal Aid, if your household has the sum of £6,200 or less left per annum, after deducting such household expenses as:

- mortgage payments;
- health contributions;
- hire purchase repayments;
- interest on other loans;
- income tax payments;
- child-minding expenses (if you are working).

Anyone in receipt of Social Welfare payments is automatically entitled to Legal Aid.

APPLYING FOR LEGAL AID

You must fill out the Means Test form, which is available from any Legal Aid Board office (see below). If you are considered to be eligible for the service, an appointment will be made for you to see one of the Legal Aid Board's solicitors. There is a charge of £3 for legal advice.

If the solicitor is of the opinion that legal action is necessary, an application will be made to the Board for a Certificate of Legal Aid. If the certificate is granted, it entitles you to be legally represented. There is a charge of £19 for legal representation.

139

THE LEGAL AID SERVICE
The Legal Aid service operates out of Law Centres, staffed by fully qualified solicitors. Because of the demand for the service, some centres may be closed to new applicants from time to time.

Note that a couple may not both use the same Legal Aid Centre in a marriage dispute. If both spouses are entitled to Legal Aid, they must be legally represented by different centres.

Legal Aid Centres are located in the following areas:
- **Dublin**: Legal Aid Board Head Office, 46 Upper Mount Street, Dublin 2; 45 Lower Gardiner Street, Dublin 2; 9 Lower Ormond Quay, Dublin 7;
- **Cork**: 24 North Mall, Cork; 96 South Mall, Cork;
- **Galway**: 5 Mary Street, Galway;
- **Kerry**: 6 High Street, Tralee;
- **Limerick**: Lower Mallow Street, Limerick;
- **Sligo**: 1 Teeling Street, Sligo;
- **Waterford**: 5 Catherine Street, Waterford;
- **Westmeath**: Northgate Street, Athlone.

It is proposed to open new centres in the following areas:
- Clondalkin;
- Finglas;
- Dundalk;
- Castlebar;
- Letterkenny.

Check with the Legal Aid Board's Head Office in Dublin for opening dates.

CRIMINAL LEGAL AID
Legal Aid is available in respect of criminal matters. Depending on your circumstances, a judge, at a preliminary hearing of the matter in the District Court, may appoint a solicitor from the Legal Aid Board to represent you.

18

LEGAL WORDS & PHRASES

ACTION: Legal proceedings.

ADJOURNMENT: The postponement of any matter in court to another date.

AFFIDAVIT: A written sworn statement given by the person who swears it, usually in front of a Commissioner for Oaths. The person making the statement is known as the Deponent.

ATTACHMENT: A court order that is issued in cases of disobedience in respect of any court order or for cases of contempt of court. The person attached may be arrested and committed to prison until the contempt is purged.

BONA FIDE: In good faith.

BRIEF: The instructions given by a solicitor to a barrister in order to enable the barrister to represent the client in legal proceedings. A brief consists of all relevant papers and documentation in the case.

CAVEAT EMPTOR: Let the buyer beware.

CHALLENGE OF JURORS: Objections made by legal representatives to jurors selected by ballot to serve on any particular jury.

COMPENSATION: A payment to make amends for loss or injury to persons or property.

CONTEMPT OF COURT: A failure to comply with any court order.

CONTRIBUTORY NEGLIGENCE: That you yourself were in some way responsible for an accident or contributed to the accident.

CONVEYANCING: The area of law dealing with the transfer of property.

COUNSEL: A practising barrister.

DPP: The Director of Public Prosecutions.

DAMAGES: Compensation.

DEFENDANT: Person against whom a legal action is being taken.

DISCOVERY OF DOCUMENTS: Procedure whereby parties involved in an action disclose to each other all necessary documents in their possession, custody or power, that relate to certain matters in the action. An application to court can be made compelling discovery of documents.

DOMICILE: The country in which a person is deemed to be permanently resident.

ESTATE: In the case of death, the sum total of a person's financial worth.

EXEMPTION CLAUSE: A clause in a contract that excludes or limits the liability of one or the other of the parties.

EXPERT WITNESS: A person with a special skill, professional qualification or technical knowledge whose opinion is admitted in evidence in court.

FATAL ACCIDENT: Where death is caused by the wrongful act or neglect of another. Entitlement to compensation is governed by the terms of the Civil Liability Act.

FULL AGE: The age of majority is now 18.

IMPOTENCE: Incapacity for normal sexual intercourse. A factor which may be taken into account in nullity of marriage cases.

INJUNCTION: A court order compelling someone to refrain from doing something or to compel them to do something.

INSTRUCTING A SOLICITOR: Giving a solicitor authority to act on your behalf in respect of legal matters.

INTERIM ORDERS: Court orders made in the course of proceedings. They are not final orders as such, and are intended to last for a limited period only, usually until the matter comes on for a full hearing.

INTESTACY: If you die intestate, you die without leaving a will. Intestacy also occurs when a will, or part of it, is deemed invalid.

JUNIOR COUNSEL: A barrister who is not a senior counsel.

JURY: A body of sworn people who are summoned to decide questions of fact in court proceedings.

JUVENILE COURTS: Special courts that deal with juvenile offenders.

MAINTENANCE: In family matters, either party to a marriage may be ordered to make periodical payments for the maintenance of the other spouse and any dependent children.

MINOR: A person under the age of 18 years.

NEGLIGENCE: The failure or omission to do something which a reasonable person would be expected to do in the circumstances of the case.

NEXT FRIEND: Any minor or person of diminished capacity who wants to bring an action must do so through the intervention of a person known as a "next friend", usually a relation.

NUISANCE: An inconvenience that materially interferes with your enjoyment of your land and property. The escape of noise, smell, smoke, fumes or vibrations, and animals from one persons property to another can constitute a nuisance in law.

NULLITY OF MARRIAGE: A decree of nullity states, in effect, that a marriage either never existed (void), or that it existed until set aside by the court (voidable). It is a civil remedy and if granted, either party is usually free to remarry under the laws of the State. A marriage can be annulled by the Church in certain circumstances. Civil nullities and Church nullities are two separate procedures.

OATHS: When you swear an oath in court you are calling on God to witness that what you say is the truth.

PARTIES: Persons suing or being sued.

PAYMENT INTO COURT: The lodging of money in court in any action for debt or damages, which a defendant says is in satisfaction of the claim.

PERSONAL REPRESENTATIVE: An executor of a will or an administrator of an estate.

PLAINTIFF: Person taking action against another party.

PLEADINGS: Written statements of fact delivered by each

143

party in a court action.

PRECEDENT: A judgement or decision of court which is cited as an authority for deciding a similar set of facts in another case.

PROBATE: Document given to the executor of a will to enable them to administer the estate of the deceased.

QUIA TIMET (Because he fears): This is a form of injunction which is used to prevent or restrain some threatened act being done, which if it was done, would cause substantial damage, and for which money would not be an adequate remedy.

REGISTRAR: Court official responsible for keeping records and drawing up court orders.

RUNNING DOWN ACTION: A court action for damages against the driver or owner of a vehicle that collides with another vehicle or person.

SENIOR COUNSEL: A Junior Counsel, after some time in practice and with expertise in a particular field, may apply to become a Senior Counsel. When a Junior Counsel becomes a Senior Counsel, they "take silk". They wear a silk gown and take precedence in court over junior barristers.

SUBPOENA: This is a summons requiring the person named in the subpoena to be present at a specified place and time, and for a specified purpose, usually as a witness in court. A subpoena duces tecum not only compels a witness to attend in court to give evidence, but also to bring along the documents specified in the subpoena.

SUMMONS: A court document asking the person to whom it is directed to come before the court.

TAXATION OF COSTS: The process of examining and if necessary reducing the bill of costs of a solicitor. The procedure is dealt with by the office of the Taxing Master in the High Court and by the County Registrar in the Circuit Court.

TRANSCRIPT: An official copy of proceedings in a court.

WARD OF COURT: A minor or a person unable to deal with their own affairs, who is placed under the protection of the court.

19

USEFUL ADDRESSES

COURTS
For addresses and telephone numbers of all courts, check under COURTS in your local directory.

PROBATE OFFICE
• Áras Uí Dhálaigh, Inns Quay, Dublin 7.
See page 61 for list of District Probate Registries.
Check local directories for telephone numbers.
• FLAC (Free Legal Advice Centres):
— 49, South William Street, Dublin 2;
— 2, Tuckey Street, Cork.

MEDIATION SERVICES
• Family Mediation Service (Under the auspices of the Department of Justice), Block 1, 5th Floor, Irish Life Centre, Lower Abbey Street, Dublin 1;
• Clanwilliam Institute, 18 Clanwilliam Terrace, Grand Canal Quay, Dublin 2.
Check local directory under MEDIATION for local mediation services.

MARRIAGE ADVISORY BODIES
• CMAC (Catholic Marriage Advisory Council, All Hallows College, Drumcondra, Dublin 9;
• Marriage Counselling Service, 24, Grafton Street, Dublin 2;
• Women's Aid-Refuge, P.O. Box 791, Dublin 6;
• Rape Crisis Centre, 78, Lower Leeson Street, Dublin 2;
• Cork Rape Crisis Service, 27A, McCurtain Street, Cork;
• The Homeless Girls' Hostel, 19 Upper Sherrard Street, Dublin 1;

- Social Welfare Information Section, Áras Mhic Dhiarmada, Store Street, Dublin 1;
- Deserted Wives Section, Phibsborough Tower, Dublin 7;
- Gingerbread, 12, Wicklow Street, Dublin 2;

OTHER ADDRESSES

- Financial Information Service Centre (FISC), 87-89, Pembroke Road, Dublin 4;
- Coolock Community Law Centre, Barry's Court Mall, North Side Shopping Centre, Coolock, Dublin 5;
- Director of Consumer Affairs, Shelbourne House, Shelbourne Road, Dublin 4;
- Irish Travel Agents Association, 32, South William Street, Dublin 2;
- An Bord Pleanála, Irish Life Centre, Abbey Street, Dublin 1;
- The Incorporated Law Society of Ireland, Blackhall Place, Dublin 7;
- The General Council of the Bar of Ireland, The Law Library, Four Courts, Dublin 7.